Why Everybody

HATES

Toronto

Startling Suggestions of a Pseudo-Scientific Study

Michael B. Davie

Manor House Publishing Inc.

National Library of Canada
Library and Archives Canada Cataloguing in Publication Data:

Davie, Michael B., 1954-
Why Everybody Hates Toronto.
Startling Suggestions of a Pseudo-Scientific study / Michael B. Davie

Includes bibliographical references.

ISBN: 0-9736477-1-X

    1.   Toronto (Ont.) – Humour. :
    2.   Toronto (Ont.) – Social conditions – 21st Century. I. Title.

FC309.3.D38 2004   971.3'541'00207
C2004-905659-X

We gratefully acknowledge the financial support of the Government of
Canada through the Book Publishing Industry Development Program
(BPIDP), Dept. of Canadian Heritage, for our publishing activities.

Acknowledgements

This book would not have been possible without the full support and co-operation of me.

I'm grateful to myself for ignoring those well-meaning individuals who tried to convince me I was wasting my time on a stupid idea.

Any free and open society accepts and encourages the full expression and exchange of ideas, no matter how asinine, juvenile or ill conceived these ideas might be. It was in this spirit that I undertook the writing of this book.

My findings may be suspect, questionable, far-fetched, perhaps even fraudulent. But they are my own and I intend to stand behind them for as long as it is convenient and desirable to do so.

Moreover, my findings are based on several hours of exhaustive research (I tire easily) engaged in a "pseudo-scientific study," a phrase some will find impressive as it contains the word "scientific."

This book is for all of you – including some Torontonians – who believe there are times when Toronto gets too carried away with its own sense of self-importance.

Ah yes, Toronto. This distant suburb of Hamilton has claimed a virtual monopoly on pomposity long enough. It's time to rise up and assert our own self-serving right to pretentiousness. Let me be the first among us with the courage to assert that right.

Finally, my thanks, as always; to my wife Philippa for standing behind me, sometimes well behind me, but behind me nonetheless.

- Michael B. Davie.

Manor House Publishing Inc.
(905) 648-2193

Why Everybody
HATES
Toronto

Michael B. Davie

Manor House Publishing Inc.

For my wife Philippa,
our children Donovan, Sarah & Ryan
& my parents, Bob & Pearl Davie

By Michael B. Davie:

All titles published by Manor House Publishing Inc., unless
indicated otherwise.

Fiction

Why Everybody Hates Toronto

Creep #
A Novel

The Late Man
A Novel

Non-fiction

Winning Ways
Vol. 2: More of the Right Stuff

Winning Ways
Vol. 1: The Right Stuff

Bushwhacked
Coping with the American Superpower

News & Features Vol. 1

News & Features Vol. 2

Following The Great Spirit
Exploring Aboriginal Belief Systems

Political Losers
In Canada, U.S., Ukraine

Distant Voices
Canadian Politics on the Outside Looking In

Canada Decentralized
Can Our Nation Survive?

Quebec and Section 33
 Why The Notwithstanding Clause Must Not Stand

Inside the Witches' Coven
Exploring Wiccan Rituals

Enterprise 2000
Hamilton, Halton, Niagara Embrace the Millennium

Success Stories BR
Business Achievement in Greater Hamilton

Hamilton: It's Happening* BR
Celebrating Hamilton's Sesquicentennial

Archival

Print History: Michael B. Davie
(Self-published, with more than 60 volumes and over 10,000 pieces of
published writings)

BR = Published by BRaSH Publishing
* = With co-author Sherry Sleightholm
# = Written under the pen name I. Murderman

Manor House Publishing Inc.
(905) 648-2193

About the author

One of Canada's most intriguing and versatile writers, Michael B. Davie is the author of business/biography books *Enterprise 2000*; the *Winning Ways* series; and *Success Stories*.

He's also the author of the humorous *Why Everybody Hates Toronto* and a number of popular novels, including *The Late Man*, and *Creep* (writing as I. Murderman).

The award-winning writer is also the author of such nationally important books as *Canada Decentralized*; and *Quebec & Section 33: Why the Notwithstanding Clause Must Not Stand*.

Other critically acclaimed books include: *Distant Voices; Political Losers, Inside The Witches' Coven, Bushwhacked, Following The Great Spirit* and the *News & Features* series of books.

Michael B. Davie is also a journalist with The Toronto Star, Canada's largest newspaper, reaching millions of readers daily.

The author has won dozens of awards for outstanding journalism. His work has also appeared in such major Canadian newspapers as the Halifax Chronicle-Herald, Montreal Gazette, Calgary Herald, Winnipeg Free Press, Edmonton Journal and Vancouver Sun.

Prior to The Star, he was an editor with The Globe and Mail, Canada's national newspaper with coast-to-coast readership.

Previous to The Globe, he spent 17 years with The Hamilton Spectator, where he won 28 journalism awards.

Prior to joining The Spectator, he spent five years with

other publications, including the daily Welland Tribune where he was a reporter, columnist and editor.

He also served two years as regional news editor for one of Ontario's largest chains of community newspapers.

Born in Hamilton in 1954, Michael B. Davie's interest in writing began in early childhood. As a pre-school child, he became withdrawn after his parents decided to divorce. He discovered his behaviour was being professionally observed when he opened the door to what he thought was a washroom and found child psychologists had been studying him through two-way mirrors.

The young child then began closely observing other children and adults, studying their interaction and watching their stories unfold.

By the late 1960s and into the 1970s, while in his teens, he was a contributing writer to counter culture publications.

He turned professional in the mid-1970s as Editor of The Phoenix serving Mohawk College of Applied Arts & Technology where he earned a Broadcast Journalism diploma.

He also holds a Niagara College Print Journalism diploma and degrees in Political Science from McMaster University where he was repeatedly named to the Deans' Honour List and won the Political Science Prize for outstanding academic achievement.

Michael B. Davie currently resides in Ancaster with his wife Philippa and their children Donovan, Sarah and Ryan.

"Despite the warm welcome, (Ernest) Hemingway had already sunk into a bad mood by the time the train arrived in Toronto. After several years of artistic freedom in Europe, the clean, sober Protestant city in which he was planning to spend the next two years reminded him all too much of the churchy lifestyle of mother Grace."

- **William Burrill,**
author, *Hemingway: The Toronto Years*.

Contents

"Everybody hates Toronto. Even people who live in Toronto hate Toronto, and if they're writers they would rather write about Uganda or Bolivia or Manitoba than the city they inhabit."

Philip Marchand,
Toronto Star Writer/Reviewer

Introduction

It's said so often that it's become something of a truism: Everybody hates Toronto.

Intrigued by this oft-heard remark, I set out to determine the underlying reasons why so many people seem to hate Toronto.

My initial goal was modest enough: I intended to write a somewhat superficial, irreverent, tongue-in-cheek book taking a few playful jabs at the city where I work as an editor and writer with The Toronto Star.

This was to be a light-hearted pseudo-scientific study, a study that some might nonetheless find impressive as it contains the word "scientific." Indeed, when it comes to the burgeoning field of bad, fake science intended primarily to entertain rather than educate, this cheeky little study was intended to be pseudo-supremo.

I wanted nothing more than to take a shallow and flippant look at Toronto, a look that did little more than skim the surface while having a few cheap laughs at the city's expense. And for the most part I succeeded. Admirably.

But something happened to this project along the way. In researching my subject, I immersed myself in Toronto culture, Toronto issues, Toronto dreams, Toronto problems, and I found my project gaining some unanticipated depth.

I also found myself gaining an appreciation for the endless complexities that make up this misunderstood city, the difficulties inherent in unchecked growth, the lack of easy answers to city woes. Indeed, there were times when I found it difficult to put aside my emerging compassion to give Toronto a good slap. But slap I did, with an array of cheap shots certain to delight Toronto-haters of all ages.

Yet, I'm embarrassed to say, this did become an educational process, flowing from an extensive two-year research effort from the fall of 2002 to the fall of 2004: In addition to combing The Toronto Star on a daily basis for insight into this city, I also perused The Globe And Mail, National Post, Toronto Sun, Hamilton Spectator and other newspapers and periodicals; I read several Toronto-oriented books, watched city-related documentaries, visited government and social agencies' websites and conducted numerous informal chats to determine why so many people hate Toronto.

I also conducted a survey of 20 participants, all of whom spoke freely about their reasons for hating Toronto.

In fairness, I found that not everyone in fact hates Toronto in its entirety. But almost everyone I spoke with hated some aspect – often several aspects – of Toronto.

And if they didn't admit to outright hatred, they confirmed there were things about Toronto that they intensely disliked.

All found things about Toronto that were annoying. Sometimes downright seriously annoying.

To any such imperfect responses I employed my "entertainment factor," a bogus scientific device that magnifies one's position to better reflect the goals of the study, all in the name of entertainment of course. And is there any cause more selflessly noble?

Truth be told, everyone I came across professed to hating something – if not everything – about Toronto.

So, after judiciously weighing all such commentary, I figured, hey, close enough. They all hate at least something about Toronto. For the purposes of our study, that means they hate Toronto. Pure and simple, my intent is to provide an insightful examination of this issue in an entertaining manner. There's no need to get bogged down with any undue scrutiny that would only suck the fun out of this exercise.

Admittedly, this isn't rocket science (or science of any kind for that matter). But the pulling together of so many insightful anecdotal comments, statistics, perceptions, news reports and analysis has created a whole that is far greater than the sum of its parts. Surprisingly, this book offers a fairly comprehensive, if decidedly informal, look at public attitudes, thoughts, biases and perceptions regarding Toronto. It also takes a heard look at some very real problems plaguing this city by the lake.

As such, it may actually contribute something of value to any examination of how negative attitudes towards Toronto are formed, and why such attitudes persist.

This book may also further an understanding among many readers as to the depth of Toronto's problems, why the city behaves as it does, and why its economic and social well-being is important to the nation as a whole. As problems are revealed, possible treatments and solutions are advanced and discussed. To that extent, even die-hard Toronto fans may find this book of considerable interest (especially if they read right through to the final chapter).

I hasten to add there was no overt attempt on my part to add any educational value to this project. I swear it was just an accident. And I apologize profusely for adding some unexpected depth to what was meant to be a purely light-hearted, frivolous pursuit of a few cheap laughs. Yet, this book manages to bring some thought-provoking insight into why the oft-repeated remark persists that everybody hates Toronto. Ultimately, this is simply my own quirky take on a truly intriguing social phenomenon.

And I hope you like *Why Everybody Hates Toronto*.

"Perhaps Wyndham Lewis, who was marooned in Toronto during World War II, said it best when he described the city as a "sanctimonious icebox," where the Presbyterians and Methodists created "a reign of terror for the toper and the whoremaster..."

William Burrill,
author, *Hemingway: The Toronto Years*.

"I don't want to live there – there are too many people and too many social problems. There's quite the snobby attitude as well – it's like they built the CN Tower to look down on the rest of us."

Laura Wysocki,
survey participant, Cambridge, Ont.

1

It's true: Everybody hates Toronto

Everybody hates Toronto.

Were truer words ever spoken?

Philip Marchand, the illustrious book reviewer and colleague of mine at The Toronto Star, is among the legions of people who readily acknowledge that "everybody hates Toronto."

Marchand asserted this simple statement of fact in a column in which he attributed a reluctance of Toronto writers to actually mention Toronto in their books. He noted: "Of course we all know the reason for this: Everybody hates Toronto."

I know what you're thinking: Marchand's a prominent book reviewer, a near-genius, and I've written a book that I'd love to have glowingly reviewed.

Therefore, you assume I'm about to launch into a lengthy suck-up passage throwing all kinds of extreme, gratuitous flattery at the man.

Well, you're wrong. I certainly don't have to sink that low. I've got some self-respect and integrity. And this book has merit that speaks for itself.

Besides, someone as talented, thoughtful and brilliant as Marchand isn't about to get taken in by a lot of flattery.

He's far too intelligent, erudite, witty, analytical and downright dapper to fall for anything like that (incidentally, the book reviewers at The Globe and Mail, National Post and all other major newspapers are also quite brilliant).

No, I was about to mention that I've heard the "I hate Toronto" phrase from many lips, not just from those as articulate and well-spoken as Marchand's.

That got me thinking: It's true. Everybody hates Toronto. But why?

I set out to answer this burning question, employing exhaustive research efforts, surveys, interviews, plus good old fashioned guess work – and plenty of it.

What evolved was an informal, pseudo-scientific study that yielded some startling findings.

Seein' The Tower

From the outset, it must be acknowledged that Toronto can certainly make a bad first impression.

One of the most striking – and offensive – features of Toronto's high-rise skyline is the CN Tower.

The world's tallest free-standing structure presents an imposing signature that boldly states: "This is Toronto."

But the tower can also have an unsettling impact on people approaching the city.

As you near Toronto, the omnipresent tower suddenly juts into view – like an abruptly raised finger.

At the base of the tower is the Skydome stadium with retractable roof, which somewhat resembles a clenched fist, with the tower itself sticking up like a single, arrogant, straightened finger – guess which one.

At a purely subliminal level, the message received is: "We're Toronto and you're not – so up yours bum-wipe!"

How rude and annoying. No wonder people hate Toronto. Up yours bum-wipe, indeed!

Of course, that's only one interpretation, however widely held it may be.

Phallic Symbol

Another interpretation is that the tower, longest in the world, is actually something of a phallic symbol.

It's as if Toronto is saying: "Look how big ours is. We've got the longest tower there is – and by tower, we mean *tower*. Is your little thing as big? No, we didn't think so…"

Here again, the Skydome completes an unfortunate image forever burned into the darkest reaches of mankind's collective psyche.

You see, the Skydome sits at the base of this huge, rigid appendage.

The dome's rounded shape is frankly somewhat reminiscent of a giant scrotum; its retractable roof folds resembling soft folds of wrinkled flesh safely containing, at the correct temperature of course, balls (and other sports paraphernalia).

As though all this somehow isn't blatantly obvious enough, the entire scene is periodically bathed in lighting – pink, flesh-coloured, lighting.

And at the huge, rigid tower's tip there flashes an urgently throbbing red light.

A charitable reading of this display might be that Toronto is simply happy to see us. *Very* happy to see us.

However, I suggest that it's just plain rude to flash one's phallic symbol in public.

Toronto may be a member of the tall tower society, but abusing a member's stature by flashing one's throbbing tip should not be considered acceptable behaviour in any societal circle.

Such disturbing appendage imagery may not seem outwardly apparent to the thousands of people struggling to get in and out of this crowded city.

But at a deeper level, these images can take hold and leave one with a vague, nagging, uncomfortable feeling – especially when it's recalled that Toronto is the "Gay Capital" of Canada.

If It's Gay It's Okay

And speaking of matters gay (clever segue no?), Toronto is home to Canada's largest gay community, a community that can, unfortunately, be quite obnoxious at times.

Before anyone accuses me of gay-bashing, let me assert that I've written many published, well-received articles on Toronto's Gay community, including sympathetic write-ups on child adoption struggles by gay couples, and the need for major advertisers, companies and retailers to "think pink," in an effort to better understand and sell to the lucrative gay market.

I've also written about prominent gay leaders and gay contributors to the wider society we share. I also view the desire of gays to marry as a basic human right and covered this issue along those lines. I wrote:

> "The happy couple exchanged gold rings and kisses in a wedding much like any other - except the Ontario government won't legally recognize it. Barbara McDowall and Gail Donnelly were joined in matrimony by Metropolitan Community Church minister Brent Hawkes on June 3, 2000.

> But the Toronto couple has none of the societal and legal status given other married people - purely be-

20

cause they're the same gender. "We're being treated like second-class citizens," says McDowall, 54. She and her 36-year-old partner simply want their marriage to be recognized in the same way as heterosexual marriages.

"Having our marriage legally recognized would mean that we belong, equally, with the rest of the people living in this country, that our relationship is valid and respected."

McDowall says also at issue is the right to choose. "Not all gays would choose to be married - in fact most probably wouldn't choose that - just like not all heterosexual couples would choose to be married. But we should all have the simple right to make that choice."

McDowall and Donnelly were among seven same-sex couples joined together by Hawkes two years ago who have mounted a legal challenge after the Ontario government refused to register the marriages. On Jan. 14, 2001, Hawkes married two more same-sex couples whose unions are also not recognized by the government and are the subject of a legal challenge... Federal Justice Minister Anne McLellan added the "one man, one woman" definition of marriage to the preamble of Bill C-23, which grants same-sex couples equal, common-law status with unmarried heterosexuals but stops short of recognizing marriage between same-sex couples.

Martha McCarthy, a lawyer with Epstein Cole who is representing the Metropolitan Community Church and some of the same-sex applicants, takes issue with the assumption heterosexual marriages alone are valid because those couples can procreate when "there is no obligation for the couple to have children."

"The message should be one of inclusiveness, that gays and lesbians are all part of the same Canadian family with the same rights as everyone else, including the right to legally marry." Cynthia Petersen, a lawyer who represented five same-sex couples in a similar legal battle in British Columbia, says... forbidding same-sex marriages is simply discrimination on the basis of gender and is a violation of equality rights under the Canadian Charter of Rights and Freedoms..." 1.

Indeed, when it comes to rights for gays, I firmly believe in equal treatment (at this point, gays can not only marry in Canada, some are already going through divorce proceedings, giving them equal access to a long-established source of great animosity. Welcome to mainstream misery).

No, the problem I have with Toronto's gay community is Gay Pride week. Throughout this "special" week, anything and everything gay is shoved in your face (well, maybe that's the wrong choice of words, but you catch my drift).

An enormous amount of ink and attention is focused on gays for the sole reason that they're gay (reverse discrimination).

The Toronto Star's Vinay Menon takes a refreshingly light-hearted approach to gay relations. In a mock letter to Toronto tourists, Menon points out: "The city has a vibrant and supportive gay and lesbian community! To learn more: Go to the intersection of Church and Wellesley. Look around! Try on that feather boa! And if you have any questions, feel free to ask one of the nice chaps sitting on the steps of any coffee-shop!" 2.

The worst aspect of Gay Pride Week is the unseemly spectacle known as the Gay Pride Parade in which a bunch of gay people march down the street to celebrate the fact that they're gay; not that they've done something truly worthwhile to warrant a parade; not that they're like Santa Claus and source of delight to children everywhere (well, let's hope not anyway); not that they're the patron saint of the Irish (other than a few errant leprechauns).

No, the big, long parade is to celebrate the fact that they're men who like to have sex with other men. Now isn't that special.

In case that basic sex message is lost on anyone, many of the "costumes" consist of g-strings and thongs and leather S&M gear and various naughty sex-wear items that leave buttocks and perhaps a few other parts exposed. Some of these outfits seem designed for surprise "wardrobe malfunctions."

Personally, when I see a parade I want to hear some youngster squeal: "Look daddy, there's Jolly Saint Nick!" Not: "Look daddy, there's a jolly gay dick!" These "costumes," and the shaking, gyrating, strutting, touching, crotch-clutching and gesturing that often goes with them, are simply obscene.

Bare-bummed, prancing homos – sometimes whipping each other's backs and asses with, well, whips – are very offensive to many people, including a lot of gays who feel it's an unseemly, obnoxious display that does nothing to improve the public image of gays or improve relations with the larger community.

A Backlash to the Back Lash

Some gays are concerned – and correctly so – that such in-your-face obscene behaviour only invites a backlash against all gays, including the majority who feel sex is a private matter that really doesn't belong on a public street in front of small children.

Think I'm exaggerating: Put the same outfits on some busty, crotch-grabbing females and hold a Straight Pride Parade (come to think of it, why isn't there a Straight Pride Parade?). Then watch irate feminists and an outraged general public take offence (I too would find such a feminine display deeply offensive each and every year I'd faithfully attend such an event).

Yet, in Toronto, if it's gay, it's okay.

Voicing any criticism gets one immediately labeled as a homophobic redneck-dullard who moves his lips when he looks at pictures.

There's a clear message in the sickly twisted, oppressively politically correct atmosphere that pervades Toronto: It's no longer enough to tolerate gays, one must also promote gayness and celebrate gayness and, to be most politically correct, perhaps even wish aloud that they too were gay, if not for that damn heterosexuality they've been cursed with.

I think I speak for a lot of people when I say there's nothing wrong with tolerating and accepting gays. That's a good thing.

But promoting the gay lifestyle? Advocating the gay lifestyle? Celebrating the gay lifestyle? Welcoming the gay lifestyle? Toronto is only a heartbeat away from making it compulsory.

I'm told that in the distant future it'll happen. In the year 2007, being gay will be mandatory in Toronto. And I'm not okay with that.

A Rich Tradition of Hatred

But the uniting of Canadians from coast to coast in their hatred for Toronto is a phenomenon – a shared cultural asset – that long predates the CN Tower and Skydome and Gay Pride Week and long commutes to the Big Smoke.

Even before there were Canadians, before Toronto was even called Toronto, before there was a city of any kind to vent at, people stood ready, willing and able to hate the place as soon as it could be conceived.

Indeed, I'm told there are actually biblical references to a future city that people aren't going to like very much.

I'd imply that city's name rhymes with Toronto, but nothing rhymes with Toronto.

And that makes it all the more difficult to slam Toronto in funny limericks, removing a potential source of satisfaction and unveiling yet another reason why people detest the place.

Virtually everyone, it seems, hates at least some aspects of Toronto, if not the city as a whole.

Personally, I hate the commute to and from this metropolis in white-knuckle, bumper-to-bumper traffic that leaves me frustrated, stressed out and gagging on exhaust fumes and pollution as I make traffic gains that are best measured in inches.

By the time I reach The Toronto Star to begin my editing shift, I'm already stressed out and exhausted from the drive in.

But the arduous commute is just one element that people truly hate about Toronto. There are clearly so many frustrations associated with Toronto that many are prone to exclaim loudly and often: "I hate Toronto!"

To understand why this hatred exists, one must first gain a sufficient understanding of Toronto and the origins of feelings of extreme dislike towards this city. And so, I offer this brief history of this much-reviled city:

A Brief History of Toronto

Toronto began some time ago and after managing to annoy a lot of people under its old name of York, it renamed itself Toronto and annoyed even more people.

It soon earned the nickname Hogtown, which Torontonians believe is owed to the city's history as a hub of the pork industry.

In fact, right from the start, Toronto (then called York) was viewed as greedy by people from Hamilton (then called Hamilton) and Port Dover (then called Port Dover).

Toronto developed into an uptight Presbyterian city that prohibited drinking and fun of any kind. It then evolved into a politically correct, corporate city and capital of Ontario that allows drinking although it's probably still secretly uneasy about you having fun of any kind.

That's it. That concludes our brief history. I don't think I've left anything out and I hope that was sufficiently brief (I do tend to run on a bit sometimes).

Marchand feels Toronto simply isn't getting enough attention.

Stating he's "not trying to make a big deal of this," and then going on to fill the better part of page with a massive opinion piece, Marchand bemoans the fact none of the books that recently won, or were even on the short list for, the Giller prize for best novel or the short list for the Governor General's Award for fiction, were actually set in Toronto. 3.

Trying To Forget Toronto

In fact, Marchand notes none of the past 10 Giller prize-winning novels were set in Toronto and you'd have to go back to Hugh Garner's Best Stories in 1963 to find a Governor General's Award-winner set in T.O. This, despite the fact that many of the winning writers actually live in the Toronto area and have for some time. 4.

Yet it seems few if any Toronto area writers actually want to write about Toronto, with the partial exception of Carol Shields who set a small part of 'Unless' in Toronto. 5.

Hog Town Shunned

Other than that, many Toronto area writers pretty much shun Hog Town.

Marchand believes he knows why: "Of course we all know the reason for this: Everybody hates Toronto. Even people who live in Toronto hate Toronto, and if they're writers they would rather write about Uganda or Bolivia or Manitoba than the city they inhabit." 6.

That's true, but the burning question is: Why? I'm here to ask that question and then answer my own question, while providing solid entertainment value in the process.

As an aside, I must state that as the author of the novel

'Friendly, Manitoba' I'm personally offended by Marchand's comment, even though I don't reside in Toronto and was only contemplating writing 'Friendly, Manitoba' when he made his remark. Now that I'm actually engaged in writing the book, I feel more offended. Way to go Philip!

To be fair, a great many Canadian writers, including Shields, Robertson Davies and Margaret Atwood, have set some of their novels at least partly in Toronto.

For this Torontonians should be grateful and stop whining. It ought to be enough that a book, any book, makes a brief reference to a character passing through Toronto while on his way to some place more culturally significant, such as Hamilton.

My own thorough research and analysis of this situation suggests that Toronto writers avoid mentioning Toronto because their experience of living in Toronto is likely unpleasant. And people, writers included, tend to avoid dwelling on unpleasant matters.

These writers probably don't like Toronto much – maybe even hate the place – and therefore rarely make mention of Toronto.

Honourable Mentions

But at least Toronto is getting *some* ink, ending a lengthy period of writers such as Arthur Hailey drawing on their Toronto experiences but recasting the setting as New York or Chicago.

But what is truly pathetic are the people who take enormous pride in watching a movie set in Chicago but filmed in Toronto: "Oh look, this fake Chicago street is actually Jarvis – isn't this wonderful?" Some of these same people take perverse pride in reading novels set elsewhere that recast as American some vaguely recognizable Toronto street or personality.

In fact, although Ernest Hemingway rarely even mentioned Canada, to many Torontonians, one of the most significant aspects of this famed, innovative American writer is that he spent the formative years of his celebrated career in Toronto in the 1920s.

But to a far greater number of Torontonians, the truly outstanding thing about Ernest Hemingway is that the man's initials spelled out the quintessential Canadian expression: "eh." This is seen as more than enough reason to launch an entire movement to make Hemingway an honorary Canadian.

Indeed, the fact that Hemingway got his start in Toronto also has some Torontonians pushing to rename the whole of Yonge Street as Heming Way.

Yet lost in all of this self-congratulatory euphoria is one very simple fact: Hemingway got his start in Toronto – but he wasn't exactly crazy about the place, finding both the beer and the rent far too expensive.

Hemingway Didn't Care For Toronto

William Burrill, author of Hemingway: The Toronto Years, recounts Hemingway's years in Toronto, toiling with the Toronto Star (something William and I can also relate to).

While with the Star, Hemingway had served in Europe as a foreign correspondent and clearly regarded his subsequent return to Toronto as a downer. As Burrill notes:

> "Despite the warm welcome, Hemingway had already sunk into a bad mood by the time the train arrived in Toronto.
>
> After several years of artistic freedom in Europe, the clean, sober Protestant city in which he was planning to spend the next two years reminded him all too much of the churchy lifestyle of mother Grace." [7]

Ouch! Commenting further on Toronto's reputation for having a stifling atmosphere, Burrill also observes:

> "Perhaps Wyndham Lewis, who was marooned

in Toronto during World War II, said it best when he described the city as a "sanctimonious icebox," where Presbyterians and Methodists created "a reign of terror for the toper and the whoremaster…" 8.

Ouch again. You might think Lewis was a little over-the-top in his recent assessment – possibly uttered in the heat of passion – offered for our enlightenment just a scant six or seven decades ago.

It seems a bit insane, you say. "A reign of terror for the toper and the whoremaster," – ridiculous, you say.

Or is it? Think of the last time you heard anyone proudly proclaim themselves as a toper or whoremaster.

Think of the last time you even heard the words "toper" or "whoremaster." That's right; Toronto has virtually wiped out these once proud titles. Way to go, Hogtown!

Politically Correct To the Max

But you don't have to go back to the Second World War to find a sanctimonious, holier-than-thou, judgemental Toronto: Hog Town today is easily the most politically correct centre on the face of the planet.

In fact, Toronto is literally the Grinch that stole Christmas: It's considered bad form – *very* bad form – to so much as mention Christmas at any time of year, but particularly at Christmas time when you're apt to offend racist people who cannot tolerate the fact that some people like to celebrate Christmas and the birth of Christ…

And one must always be very sensitive to the sensibilities of racist people who cannot tolerate the fact that some people like to celebrate Christmas and the birth of Christ.

The city government and many employers take particular pride in "proving" to everyone that they're not prejudiced against people from various foreign ethnicities by making a fuss over the religious holidays of others, no matter how obscure.

It's particularly special if you wish someone a Happy Chanukah or a Rockin' Ramadan but very wrong to wish someone a Merry Christmas.

Toronto recently renamed its Christmas tree a "holiday" tree and it seems the only acceptable Christmas greeting is one such as "happy holidays" or "season's greetings," which makes no mention of the word Christmas.

I wonder when the Hindus, Jews and all other religious groups are going to make their religious holidays generic events so as not to offend Christians and other religious groups? I'm still waiting. But I'm not holding my breath.

Have Yourself a Very Merry Whatever

In Christmas 2003, one corporate Toronto secretary issued a warm-hearted email invitation to attend a Christmas party.

This happy email was followed a short time later by another email from the same secretary, who had apparently been spoken to and was now apologizing for slipping up.

She was now correcting herself and re-inviting everyone to a "holiday party."

Makes you wonder how many attended this politically correct event.

Personally, I'm not big on joyless, generic, meaningless events that celebrate nothing. But that's just me. Some people really like that kind of stuff.

There's often no escaping politically correctness at home either. Faced with paying $300,000 or more for a fixer-upper house, many Torontonians opt for less expensive $200,000 condominium apartments, only to find themselves dealing with politically correct condo boards.

These righteous boards prohibit unit-owners from putting

up a festive Christmas wreath on their door – because that door can be seen by other owners in the hallway, and we wouldn't want to offend them with some Christmas cheer now would we?

Hyphenating Canadians

In Toronto, if you're not Liberal, you're not listening. That's Liberal with a capital L, as in Liberal Party. Except this party isn't so much liberal as it is opportunistic.

The provincial Conservatives under Bill Davis were pretty much Liberals in Tory clothing, borrowing their policies from the Liberal platform, while Davis's successor, Mike Harris seemed to freely borrow every failed policy ever attempted in the United States.

But Liberals are the most ardent borrowers. Lacking ideas of their own, the Liberals blatantly steal the platform planks of rival parties such as the Conservatives and the New Democratic Party.

Some of these ideas are right wing, some are left wing, but all enjoy a degree of support from the electorate.

Putting it charitably, it's pragmatic, practical politics that to some degree truly reflects the will of the people.

Put more crassly, it's pandering to the masses, the purchasing of popularity, the buying of votes.

Another way the Liberals buy votes is through immigration ethnicity and the wooing of support from visible minorities.

The prevailing tact operates on the philosophy that immigrants travel across the world to move to Canada so that they can hang onto their old culture and resist adapting to Canada.

That the reverse is true – that they actually came here to become Canadians and adopt our culture as their own – is of no consequence.

Toronto, more so than just about any other Canadian city, delights in ghettoizing the newcomers into various ethnic groups.

And as part of the Liberal vote-buying strategy, these various ethnic groups are then catered to with funding to pay them for holding a parade or an event that displays their old culture.

This unwanted catering arrives with great fanfare, despite the fact that most of them would rather leave the past in the past and concentrate on the Canadian present and future.

They just want to get on with their lives.

But just when they're starting to feel truly Canadian, there's always a bureaucrat or the media to remind them that they're a visible minority.

The vote-buying strategy also fosters the pretence that these groups have special (read expensive) needs and issues that must be urgently dealt with.

As a visible minority, someone out there must be discriminating against them.

And if they haven't noticed anyone exhibiting prejudice, a costly study should be able to find some obscure incident or impression that can be blown up to justify the undertaking of the costly study. And more dollars will be needed to rectify this situation.

This, of course, is followed by a sanctimonious report that immediately decries the perceived existence of widespread discrimination and prejudice in our society.

The report and its politically correct champions hastily label as racist anyone who questions unsafe or bizarre foreign customs, with the exception of the time-honoured practice by some groups of stoning adulterous women to death.

Canadian Culture Doesn't Count

Overall, the message is always the same.

The people who just arrived have cultural traditions that must be respected and nurtured and heavily funded, no matter how much they might seem to be at odds with Canadian culture, which after all doesn't really count.

Even third generation Canadians who have darker skin can't escape the ghettoization efforts.

Try as they might to simply be accepted as Canadians, visible minorities are constantly divided up into little groups that society is somehow failing to fully service.

It seems we're always falling short and letting them down. But here's a few more million dollars and an apology and a request – more of an indirect suggestion or inference really – that you consider voting Liberal.

Anyone who questions the idea of a soldier wearing a cloth turban instead of a helmet or objects to a Mountie wearing a turban instead of the time-honoured RCMP Stetson is dismissed as a redneck and racist. It's the Liberal way.

What Black Community?

Occasionally these Canadians will assert their right to be Canadians.

Sometimes it takes the form of someone in the "Black Community" pointing out that there is no "black community," any more than there is a white community and that this racist notion ignores the fact that many blacks were born here while others came from 50 different countries with completely different cultures.

Their only similarity is the most superficial one possible: the colour of their skin. But the Liberal ghettoization efforts continue.

Of course, not everyone in Toronto votes Liberal. But enough do to give the city an air of arrogant self-righteousness.

Not that the Liberals have a monopoly on segregating Canadians.

The Tories in particular also like to divide Canadians, only in their case, it's usually along economic lines with policies that ensure the rich get richer and the poor get poorer. And middle-income Canadians get stuck with paying the bill for this misguided largesse.

Hand-in-hand with all of this nonsense is Toronto's over-arching desire to be politically correct at all times.

This is necessary if you want to indulge in a time-honoured habit of looking down on all other parts of the country that are not as politically correct – and therefore not as advanced or enlightened – as you are.

The effect of constantly striving to be politically correct, to speak in politically correct ways and to think in politically correct terms isn't always easy.

After all, what's politically correct today may be politically incorrect tomorrow.

But generally, a helpful rule of thumb suggests that if a measure goes against the interests of a majority of Canadians, it's usually safe to assume it's politically correct.

Watch What You Say

It's enough to give one pause, to make one avoid speaking freely, to limit one's conversational discourse to broad pronouncements that all minority groups and cultures are wonderful and contribute enormously to our cultural fabric and we should do more for them, perhaps starting with substantial funding.

It's also enough to make it quite difficult to relax and have fun (try telling a joke that's actually funny without it being at the expense of a minority group).

Toronto doesn't have a monopoly on political correctness (Ottawa deserves its own book). But it's here that the politically correct truly flourish at the expense of all others who prefer thinking for themselves and weighing arguments on the basis of merit, rather than following a preconceived rigid thought pattern.

And nowhere is the politically correct attitude more pervasive, more self-righteously intense than in Toronto's uptight, overly serious office environment.

Jokes Corrected

Here, any half-joking remark is sure to be 'corrected' by a judgemental co-worker in an intensely competitive setting in which no-one dares leave 10 minutes early on a Friday lest they be labelled a slacker.

Here, self-regulated and self-censured speech patterns are in full vogue.

Politically correct statements meet with approving nods and illicit more stale politically correct statements from others who meet with more approving nods.

It's a game with rigid rules, void of fun, a workaholic ritual that accepts you for who you really aren't.

The important this is to make sure you always get on the high moral ground (usually whatever goes against the majority in favour of a minority group or religion).

And don't forget to nod approvingly whenever anyone makes a politically correct statement – and frown whenever they don't.

Then make some astute politically correct statements of your own to further win favour.

It's all about keeping up appearances.

So what if it looks like you're walking around with a pole shoved up your ass (notice I said pole, not Pole, as I have no intention of slighting Polish people who are uniformly wonderful and contribute enormously to our cultural fabric and we should do more for them, perhaps starting with substantial funding).

A Humble City State

Toronto managed to arouse a plethora of hostile feelings when it began making noises that it would like to be treated by upper levels of government as though it was some sort of city state. Commenting on Toronto's vainglorious bid for special status, the Ottawa Citizen opined:

> "If there was a gold medal for complaining, the city of Toronto would win it. Toronto is indignant that the province considers it to be just another city... Toronto thinks its officials should have the right to meet mano-a-mano with (Premier) Dalton McGuinty when discussing municipal-provincial relations and the future of our cities. Instead, Mr. McGuinty has been hinting that his preference is to negotiate through the Association of Municipalities of Ontario (AMO), of which Toronto is but a member." 9.

The Citizen editorial then expresses mock outrage: "Imagine! Rather than getting its very own seat at the table, Toronto would have to share with the likes of Ottawa, London, Owen Sound and Sudbury. Quelle Insulte! Toronto does not think much of the AMO." 10.

Suggesting Toronto views itself as a swank department store amid five-and-dimes, the Citizen noted: "The AMO is holding its annual meeting in Ottawa and it speaks volumes that Toronto Mayor David Miller chose this week to take his vacation." 11.

Toronto a Distinct Society?

Noting Toronto Councillor Howard Moscoe is dismissing the premier's informal pledge to address Toronto concerns as they arise and wants something "enshrining in legislation," the Citizen wondered is Toronto wants a law passed declaring it a city state or a Distinct Society...In any event, it's time for Toronto to stop whining." 12.

We'll examine this special status issue a little more closely later on. But for now, let's just say that it ticks a lot of people off.

And so, we've already examined a number of reasons why people hate Toronto, ranging from an insistence on preventing immigrants from becoming Canadians and the constant isolating and ghettoizing of our fellow citizens, to the holier-than-thou politically correct set, the dismissal of our own culture, and the widespread disrespect for Christian customs and beliefs in a zealous effort to suck up to other religions.

And its attempts to achieve special treatment from provincial and federal governments, attempts viewed by many as a pompous effort to achieve city state status.

But as we're about to discover there are more – many more – reasons why people hate Toronto.

It's time know to visit our survey and look at the anecdotal evidence it brings to this most compelling of questions: Why indeed does everybody hate Toronto?

"Toronto is too damn busy. There are people everywhere. The pace of life is too fast. It's uncomfortable."

Karen Sibley,
Survey participant, Hamilton, Ontario.

"I suppose what I hate about Toronto is the attitude. They think they're so great – I can't stand their 'we're-the-centre-of-the-universe' attitude."

Joan Gibson,
Survey participant, Hamilton, Ontario

2

Survey Says…

An impromptu Canada Day 2004 survey of Canadian celebrants in Hamilton revealed a wealth of reasons why people hate Toronto.

It should be said that not all participants hated everything about Toronto.

But all hated something – usually several things – about the nearby metropolis that takes hours to reach despite being 45-minutes away.

We – and by we I mean me – came across a full range of emotions from intense dislike to absolute hatred. And everything in between.

If by chance we encountered anyone who simply disliked Toronto, we stood ready with our "entertainment factor" a non-scientific device to exaggerate their feeling into one of hatred, purely for entertainment purposes.

For the most part, we did not have to use this device. Virtually everyone hated something about Toronto.

All participants hailed from Hamilton and other south-central Ontario communities. They were asked: "Why do you hate Toronto?"

Although some protested that this was a leading question that presupposed a certain viewpoint, they then went on to confirm that they do indeed hate a number of things about Toronto.

All told, at least 20 people were surveyed and it's believed that all responded as honestly and forth-rightly as they were able. Their responses follow:

Laura Wysocki: "Toronto can be quite disgusting sometimes. It's one of the few places where people will urinate and pleasure themselves on the street. It's a violent city also. I don't want to live there – there's too many people and too many social problems. There's quite the snobby attitude as well – it's like they built the CN Tower to look down on the rest of us."

Brad Muir: "The traffic congestion is awful. And Toronto has some very aggressive drivers who can cause a lot of problems.

Jim Sibley: "I don't like diesel with my dog. What do I mean by that? I'm saying I don't like to taste diesel or gasoline fumes when I order a hot dog from one of those street venders. It's bad enough having to breathe in Toronto, having to suck in their air pollution every time you breathe, without having to taste it in your food. I live near industry in Hamilton so I'm used to some pollution but the extreme air pollution in Toronto is disgusting.

Wendy Sibley: "I hate Toronto because it's Toronto, a big cold city full of strangers in a rush to get somewhere else. I also hate the violence there, the street gangs – and the Argos suck."

Linda Puder: "Toronto has gotten way too big and impersonal. There's too many people and too much traffic. I was born and raised in Toronto, but would I live there again? No. It's too large now. And there's too many crimes and too many killings."

Marty Wilson: "I hate Toronto's traffic."

Phyllis Lankester: Toronto is too crowded downtown. Other parts of it are nice – some nice houses and neighbourhoods – but generally, the streets are crowded. There are very busy streets and the noise factor downtown is just unbelievable."

Keith Lankester: "I especially hate Toronto when I have to drive from Hamilton to Toronto. I hate the traffic congestion in Toronto. I also hate Toronto because it rules all of Canada and it alienates Western Canadians."

Dale Roksa: "The parking rates in Toronto are just so unbelievably expensive compared to anywhere else in Canada. It costs a fortune to park in Toronto – if you can find a parking spot. It's also weird driving there because there's too many crazy people around. I once had a man stop my car for no reason – then he just walked away."

Karen Sibley: Toronto is too damn busy. There are people everywhere. The pace of life is too fast. It's uncomfortable."

Joan Gibson: I suppose what I hate about Toronto is the attitude. They think they're so great – I can't stand their 'we're-the-centre-of-the-universe' attitude."

Pearl Davie: I quite like visiting Toronto – I'm just glad I don't have to live there. The traffic is difficult for anyone who has to drive a car and it is a big source of pollution. Toronto also seems to get a lot of funding from the provincial government while Hamilton needs funding a lot more but doesn't seem to get any.

David Gibson Jr.: "Torontonians are kind of like Americans – they're kind of obnoxious. I can't pull off the highway there without getting my windows cleaned twenty-five times by homeless "squeegee kids," in their twenties and thirties. It's so busy, so packed with people in Toronto that you can't get anywhere anymore. And the traffic jams are unreal. It once took us an hour to get to our destination just five blocks away. The parking fees are outrageous and the overall cost of living in Toronto is ridiculous."

Colleen Gibson: "Highway traffic is often blocked up for miles, and everything's so expensive in Toronto for no reason."

Joe (real name withheld by request): I hate Toronto but unfortunately I have to business with companies in Toronto so I don't want my name used. I know from dealing with so many Toronto people that it takes both the husband and wife working just to make ends meet and there's a lot of latch-key kids in Toronto, who are left on their own all day. It isn't right. Life shouldn't be that expensive, it shouldn't be so hard just to get by – but it is in Toronto. It's like Toronto is punishing you for living there."

Tim (real name withheld by request): I know a lot of people in Toronto, so I don't want them reading my name and feeling insulted. But the fact is, they're all a bunch of workaholics in Toronto. There's so many kiss-asses that put in the unpaid extra hours in Toronto that if you're not a kiss-ass yourself, you can't get ahead. It's not how I'd want to live."

Dave Gibson Sr.: "I was born in Toronto – that's probably why I don't like the place now, it's changed so much. I haven't been to Toronto in a long time and I've no desire to go there because it's so big now. It's too big a pain in the ass to get around. But they're smart. Unlike Hamilton they take everything the province and federal government offers them."

Michael B. Davie: "Sure there are things I hate about Toronto – the traffic, the lengthy commute, the workaholic attitudes, the congestion. But what I really hate most is having my privacy invaded by surveys such as this one."

Gene Mason: "Just driving there is an unpleasant, time-consuming experience. The (highway) 401 should be shut down it's so useless. And why do you have to pay to use the 407? It's an outrage that you have to pay a toll to use a provincial highway our tax dollars have already paid for. All the big banks have moved to Toronto – including the ones that used to be in Hamilton and other parts of the country – so now Toronto can lord it over everybody as the financial centre of Canada. There's also too many gangs and crime going on there. It's not safe to walk the streets in Toronto. They've got a great location; right on the lake, but they block the view with a bunch of condos. It's ridiculous."

Donovan Davie: "It's very inconvenient to get from one place to another in Toronto and I think the people there look down on anyone who isn't from there. It's a hard to start off there and get ahead because it's so expensive to live or work there."

Philippa Davie: "I'm glad I don't commute to Toronto or have to drive there and I avoid driving anywhere near Toronto. If we're going up north, we'll take the highways that bypass Toronto even if it costs more – it's a lot less stressful and it's worth it for the peace of mind."

In addition to soliciting the views of survey participants, I also engaged fellow train travellers in discussions on Toronto.

And I overheard a number of frank conversations that went to the heart of this phenomenon. For example:

Overheard on the GO Train:

"I'm over by Jarvis Street and there's these big corporate buildings in the neighbourhood – Molson's and other big companies. You wouldn't believe the Mercedes and BMW and Lexus cars going by.

So why do I have to deal with homeless people in that same neighbourhood hitting me up for spare change?

Why can't some of these rich dudes slow down and give these poor people some coffee money? They don't even see them. They live in their own little rich-boy world.

But people are living on the streets in poverty. There's crime everywhere. The city is just choked no with high-rise buildings – condos everywhere – and people packed together like rats.

Not like when I was growing up here. There

weren't all these buildings and people and crime and poverty and social problems everywhere. I don't think those rich dudes are going to be able to ignore this forever.

Sooner or later the problems are going to sneak up on them and bite them good.

Meanwhile, why do I have to be the one getting hit on all the time for spare change?"

And there you have it. A great deal of animosity directed at Toronto, virtually all of it tinged with a sense of sadness that a potentially great city is seemingly oblivious to so many problems – and has squandered so many opportunities to get it right.

It's important to note that none of the opinions presented were motivated by anything other than a desire to share one's honestly held viewpoint.

These responses were from ordinary Canadians reflecting on their sources of frustrations with the behemoth that is Toronto. As such these are perceptions that are not unique to the individuals expressing them.

Indeed we – and by we I mean me – encountered very similar viewpoints from many different quarters. There are many things about Toronto that truly annoy people.

And subsequent chapters in this book will continue to delve into many of the major sources of dissatisfaction with Toronto.

"I'm glad I don't commute to Toronto or have to drive there and I avoid driving anywhere near Toronto. If we're going up north, we'll take the highways that bypass Toronto even if it costs more – it's a lot less stressful and it's worth it for the peace of mind."

Philippa Davie, survey participant, Ancaster.

"Just driving there is an unpleasant, time-consuming experience. The (highway) 401 should be shut down it's so useless. And why do you have to pay to use the 407? It's an outrage that you have to pay a toll to use a provincial highway our tax dollars have already paid for."

Gene Mason, survey participant, Hamilton.

"The parking rates in Toronto are just so unbelievably expensive compared to anywhere else in Canada. It costs a fortune to park in Toronto – if you can find a parking spot. It's also weird driving there because there's too many crazy people around. I once had a man stop my car for no reason – then he just walked away."

Dale Roksa, survey participant, Hamilton.

"The traffic congestion is awful. And Toronto has some very aggressive drivers who can cause a lot of problems.

Brad Muir, survey participant, Hamilton.

3

Driving us Crazy

Toronto drivers are truly crazy. They cut you off in traffic and give you the finger when you try to save both your lives by not crashing into them. And, to continue generalizing, they'll risk an accident rather than let you into the traffic stream when you're entering a highway. But those are just mild examples. Some drivers are crazier than others. Reporting on a weekend police blitz on drivers, the Toronto Star's Bob Mitchell described a bizarre police pullover:

> "None of them should have been in the car. Waved over by highway police for a baby-seat inspection, the driver of a black cavalier at first tried to duck in behind a trailer and switch positions. It turned out the car's plates and licence sticker were stolen and the driver had no insurance. What's more, the man and his female passenger had suspended licences, and he was wanted on outstanding warrants ranging from theft to assault. Plus he 'wasn't supposed to be within 100 metres of the female in the car, as the result of an earlier court order,' OPP-Sergeant Cam Woolley said. The car was towed… the man was arrested." 1.

Other bad drivers nabbed in the blitz included a 24-year-old man who said he was driving at twice the speed limit because highway driving made him nervous so if he drove really fast he'd spend less time on the highway. 2.

Another speeder – again doing twice the speed limit – was weaving in an out of traffic at high speeds in slipper foggy road conditions. After he crashed into a guardrail, police charged him with dangerous and impaired driving and driving with an open bottle of liquor. 3.

And, a 27-year-old driver and his four children were found in a vehicle with a broken driver's seat that one of the children had to steady as he drove. None of the people in the car wore a seatbelt. 4.

Yet another driver's car was towed away because its windshield was held together by duct tape. 5.

Mitchell goes on to note that the impromptu inspections on series 400 highways in the Toronto area resulted in more then 650 people being charged with driving infractions and nearly 200 unsafe vehicles were finally removed from the highways. 6.

Think about it for a moment: Hundreds of unsafe vehicles on the road and enough reckless drivers to warrant 650 charges – and that's who we're sharing the road with.

It's enough to make me look nervously over my shoulder – if there wasn't someone trying to cut me off right now while giving me the finger.

Worse still are the drivers who enter highways at speeds that wouldn't be out of place in a driveway.

Then they continue to drive as slowly as possible, backing traffic up for miles, fraying the nerves of other drivers, and, ultimately encouraging the kind of reckless response from others that causes accidents.

What can be done about this madness?

It's rare that politicians have the answer and Ontario Transportation Minister Harinder Takhar is no exception. Takhar stupidly suggested he's considering ordering all drivers in the province to get retested or lose their driver's licence. Such a move would be nothing more than a blatant tax grab.

It would also subject all Ontario drivers to needless inconvenience and bother while doing nothing to improve safety. As The Toronto Star observed in an editorial:

> "An updated licence would do nothing to prevent bad drivers from going back to their dangerous habits. A freshly minted licence won't prevent idiots from speeding, tailgating or weaving all over the highway." 7.

Of course, speeding and weaving infractions assume you can actually move on the highway.

For much of the day, Toronto's major thoroughfares are virtual parking lots, where progress in bumper-to-bumper traffic is literally measured in inches.

If you're headed for north Toronto – or want to avoid this traffic-choked city altogether – you can take the much faster Highway 407, a new roadway built with taxpayers dollars.

And these same taxpayers must now pay tolls for the privilege of using a highway we've already paid for at least once.

Highway 407 presents the opportunity to pay for the same stretch of pavement again and again and again, with your exorbitant fees going not to your government, but to a private consortium that's focused on profit not service and certainly not fairness.

In its defence, the consortium can truthfully say that it's increased toll rates by "only" 200 per cent in the last five years alone – and they have 94 years left to run in their road lease. Who knows how much motorists will be gouged to use our own highway in years to come.

Far away from Highway 407, in downtown Toronto, gridlock continues unabated, fraying tempers and causing life-threatening delays for ambulances trying to reach emergency rooms as fast as possible in rush-hour traffic.

How ridiculously slow is Toronto traffic? Toronto Star reporters Angus Loten and Frank Calleja report:

> "In rush-hour traffic, (bicycle-rider Fraser) Smith clocked the fastest time in a three-way challenge between a cyclist, a driver and transit rider, all commuting from North York to the downtown core." 8.

And, adding insult to injury are other nuisance factors such as parking, gas and vehicle maintenance afflicting motorists who are routinely overtaken by people on bikes.

Anti-auto environmentalists always advocate the public transit option, arguing everything would be fine if we just left our cars at home. But in fact, public transit isn't much of an option if you're commuting any distance to Toronto.

First of all, unless you live next to the train station, you have to drive some distance to get there – through rush-hour traffic.

In my case, I rise at 6 a.m. so I can leave my home in Ancaster by 7 and spend a half an hour in rush-hour traffic making what should be a 15-minute (only in the non-rush-hour time zone of 2 a.m. to 4 a.m.) trip to the Burlington GO Train station.

The nearest parking spot is a half-mile from the train, so I walk fast to make the 7:45 a.m. train.

The train takes an hour to complete what should only be a half-hour trip, arriving at 8:45 a.m. at Union Station in Toronto. It then takes me another 15 minutes to walk from Union Station to my desk at The Toronto Star.

Having just completed a two-hour commute, I'm now ready to start my day, a day that actually began three hours earlier. And at the "end" of my day, it'll take me another two-hour commute to get home to complete my 12-hour day.

The drive-train-walk routine really isn't any faster than driving alone (in fact it takes less time to drive in – even during rush-hours).

But it does save me constantly filling the family van with gas to sit in traffic for two hours or more.

It also saves me parking costs and some of the upkeep costs on my vehicle.

However, the train is not an option whenever I work a night shift as the trains run a full hour apart during the evening, meaning that if I wrap up my shift at midnight and miss the train, I won't be getting home until 2 a.m. – in which case, there's no point going home at all.

Nor is the train or bus much of an option for many suburbanites. Brampton resident Evangeline Moffat recounts her experiences taking the train into Toronto, a trip her children now refuse to make because "it's too far," and takes far too long. As Moffat recalls:

> "I took GO Transit to a recent Toronto lunch… I raced out of my house shortly after breakfast – 9:35 a.m. – to catch the only post-rush hour bus that gets me into the city before 1 p.m. Noting that it takes far too long to take Brampton transit to the GO Bus stop, Moffat drove to a GO stop at a shopping mall, only to find the bus to Union Station wasn't running and she'd have to take the train instead. "Finally, at 10:48 a.m., the train pulled into Union. I still had an hour to kill before lunch. But taking GO means abiding by its schedule, not mine… driving into town is easier." 9.

Moffat notes that she now often avoids going into Toronto for socializing, entertainment or anything else because trip, whether by public transit or car, simply isn't worth the hassle. 10.

It's likely many suburbanites feel the same way. They spend as little time in Toronto as possible due to the draining, exhausting, time-consuming hassle of getting there and back.

For example, if you miss the bus in Mississauga, you may have to wait an hour for the next one – and this is considered an efficient alternative to car travel? Public transit is too limited to be much of an option in many cases. And people who might otherwise experience Toronto and spend their money their instead spend their time closer to home.

Parking Problems

If you can find a parking space in Toronto (most of the surface lots are being replaced by condos), expect to pay dearly for it. Parking anywhere near the city's entertainment district (commonly defined as "all of Toronto") can cost you more than the movie or live performance you came to see.

Daily rates can run as high as $60. Many lots charge exorbitant rates by the half-hour "or part" which means you can pay $20 to park five minutes.

Valet parking is so expensive it's not an option for all but the richest among us.

And monthly parking passes? Fuggedaboutit. As the Toronto Star's Kevin McGran reports:

"Toronto is one of the most expensive cities in North America to park your car, an international survey concludes, and experts say it will only get more expensive as condominium development snaps up vacant lots... Toronto is the most expensive city in Canada and the 10th most expensive city in North America in which to buy a monthly unreserved parking pass. It costs Toronto drivers an average of $268 (all amounts in Canadian dollars)... ahead of Calgary and Los Angeles (both around $252).   11.

But of course you're getting real value for your money sent, right? I mean, you get to park your vehicle yourself in a pothole riddled lot and... and... And nothing.

There are no services. Not even security. The only time

anyone ever broke into my family van was while I was parked in Toronto – ten feet from the manned attendant booth. You park your own vehicle. You do all the work, and some guy who speaks little English and lives on the lot – in a very tiny house with a phone and TV but no bathroom – takes your money and gives it to some fat cat who parks for free and drives an SUV.

You can't even get mad at the attendants: They're just hapless pawns, paid minimum wage with the added incentive of a free tiny booth-house "conveniently located close to everything."

My wife Philippa and I and another couple are still recovering from the shock of paying parking rates that exceeded the cost of our Jethro Tull concert tickets.

On objecting to the attendant that we only wanted to rent a parking space, not buy it, he protested: "It's not me, man. It's the suits. It's the suits gouging everybody. I'm just a guy in a booth, man. Please don't hit me again."

The only free parking to be found in Toronto is on the Gardner Expressway itself during rush hours. At these times, you can leave your vehicle, go for a bite to eat, perhaps take in a show, and return to your car in time to find the moron behind you honking his horn because you haven't moved two-inches forward. I exaggerate… but only a little.

Montrealer: What's Torontonian's favourite expression?
Innocent bystander: I don't know. I give up.
Montrealler: T.G.I.M.
Innocent bystander: T.G.I. M???
Montrealer: Yeah, Thank God It's Monday.

"They're all a bunch of workaholics in Toronto. There's so many kiss-asses that put in the unpaid extra hours in Toronto that if you're not a kiss-ass yourself, you can't get ahead. It's not how I'd want to live."

Tim (real name withheld by request) survey participant, Hamilton.

4

Thank God it's Monday

For too many Torontonians the work-life is all-consuming. Their lives are at the office. Anything else – vacations, family – are just distractions.

They live for work, for the rat race, for jumping back on the treadmill, for chasing elusive promotions that promise even longer work hours.

Fun be damned, it's time to work.

This work ethic run amok reflects badly on the rest of us who do take vacations and think of our lives in human rather than career terms.

People hate Toronto for making them feel like slackers for wanting to relax with a beer as often as humanly possible.

These joyless, workaholic Torontonians have not gone unnoticed by their office counterparts in the much more liveable city of Montreal.

There, the standard joke is: "What's a Torontonian's favourite expression? Answer: Thank God it's Monday."

Work for the sake of work. Work as a substitute for life. As The Toronto Star's Books reviews page opined:

> "Torontonians have a reputation among more civilized Canadians, fairly earned or not, as folks who aren't very good at relaxing, even in summer, for fear someone else will pass them by." [1.]

It's reached the point where major newspapers feel obliged to run articles instructing Torontonians how to relax, leave the office at the office, leave the cell phone behind.

Race towards an Early Grave

Although it's obvious to most non-Torontonians, the experts also urge workaholics to unplug and enjoy their holidays by not taking the laptop computer, cell phone, pager and Internet with you to the beach or cottage, not checking messages while on vacation, unplugging from the rat race. [2.]

Workaholic Torontonians have to be reminded even to take vacations, to interrupt time-honoured habits of working long hours without a break. They fear taking a vacation will be seen as slacking off, and therefore dangerous to one's career. But working incessantly is dangerous to one's heath. As the Toronto Star's Judy Gerstel reports:

> "The traditional two-week vacation has gone the way of the teletype – and in part for the same reason. The technology and pace of the 21st century has tethered us to such a fast-paced electronic employment and family life treadmill that it takes almost superhuman effort to break away for more than a few days... More and more it just seems easier to surrender to routine and forget about getting away. But that's exactly what we should not be doing. Vacations are crucial for emotional and physical health, feelings of well-being and peak performance on the job, say researchers and psychologists..." [3.]

Indeed virtually all mental health experts say vacations are necessary, that people should not feel guilty about taking earned time off, that they should completely separate themselves from the work environment for a full break, that they should avoid thinking about work and avoid worrying if taking a break limits their career path.

They should relax and have fun rather than worry if their break is perceived by others as laziness.

Yet statistics show a third of Canadians – and half of all business executives – forego taking vacations, returning $8-billion in unused holiday time to employers each year.

Compare this workaholic nonsense with European countries where long lunches are the norm, as are month-long breaks. In contrast, Toronto is Corporate Coronary Central.

Although this extreme work ethic problem isn't unique to Toronto, this city, more than any other, embodies the corporate workaholic lifestyle. Toronto is the undisputed corporate capital of Canada. The city is steeped in business jargon, saturated in business culture, awash in business attitudes and values.

Toronto Controls Our Lives

The vast majority of head offices of major corporations are located in the Greater Toronto Area, and given the city's high percentage of business executives, foregoing vacations is considered somewhat normal here.

Even those few big firms that have their head office somewhere else – say Winnipeg – often have a Toronto "branch" office that dwarfs the so-called "head office' and the branch location often becomes the source of major decision-making, effectively making it a head office in all but name.

Most often, the head office is referred to as "the Toronto office," the place where decisions are made to the benefit of the Toronto office – and perhaps no one else.

Get a new work schedule that ignores your daycare needs? Find yourself "multi-tasking" to assist a hiring freeze? Lose your job as a cost-cutting measure to pay for an asinine merger? Chances are the decisions behind these changes were made by head office, the Toronto office.

This is a huge source of resentment. People who live hundreds, sometimes even thousands of miles (or kilometres – reader's choice) away can suddenly find their branch plant job is no more, thanks to a decision made by the Toronto office to downsize or in the newest parlance, "right-size," as though your job was actually just a horrible mistake in the first place that only now – good news! – is being "corrected" through the elimination of one's livelihood.

Most people – including Torontonians – would not want to inflict job loss on another human being. Most people would search for other options, other alternatives that spared their fellow man the dehumanizing, demoralizing and soul-destroying punishment of families losing their sole source of income.

But corporations aren't people and they literally don't care at all how much they might be hurting people in their quest for an enhanced bottom line.

Psycho Corporate Culture

Corporations are however legal entities with legally protected rights and freedoms. But they have few, if any, real responsibilities. As such, corporations can be viewed as an individual without a conscience, with their closest human equivalent being a cold, calculating and heartless psychopath.

Discussing the work of the late former federal cabinet minister and intellectual Eric Kierans, Toronto Star columnist Richard Gwyn observed that Kierans warned: "corporations are soulless and that as they take over the world they are making it a soulless place." 4.

Much like psychopaths, firms are singularly self-interested, irresponsible and without remorse.

Firms have no empathy, accept little or no responsibility for their actions and have no problem acting in ways that harm people and the environment. They relate superficially to others, making slick public relations statements to justify and praise purely selfish actions. 5.

Firms can, and do, kill jobs, livelihoods and whole communities without shedding a single tear of remorse. They're perfect, unfeeling, immoral psychopaths interested solely in accumulating wealth – and eliminating anyone who gets in the way.

And many of these psychopathic entities are immortal giants that seduce new generations of businessmen who travel in committees and make horrific, life-destroying decisions that no one individual can be held accountable for.

With so many corporations residing in Toronto, corporate culture has become somewhat synonymous with Toronto civic culture.

Toronto is seen as the core champion of an inhuman, performance-driven, big business attitude that runs roughshod over ordinary people.

Toronto is the embodiment of Corporate Canada.

Big Banks

Toronto is also the nation's leading financial centre and home to most of the much-hated big banks, which are essentially just like any other psycho corporations except they control your money and charge huge "service" fees.

Remember when you could put your money in a savings account and actually save some money and watch it grow?

Remember too when the banks paid you a decent amount of interest to compensate for the fact that they were borrowing your money to invest at even higher returns and keeping the difference as well earned profit?

That golden era vanished in the 1980s when the big banks stupidly loaned money – and plenty of it – to third world countries that never had any hope of paying it back.

When these same impoverished countries defaulted on their loans (big surprise), the banks covered their losses by making us pay.

An unholy onslaught of service charges by millions of Canadians would raise enough revenue to counter the massive losses from ill-fated Third World loans.

Once these loans were covered, the banks continued with their usurious service charges and actually bragged about the massive profits they 'earned' at are expense. And Toronto is home to most of these parasitic leeches.

Now your return of 4 cents is slightly offset by $27.50 in service charges.

Think of the times you've personally felt frustrated even victimized by big corporations, big banks, big government – and where do they all reside, if not Toronto?

Western Alienation

This in large part explains the Western alienation feelings harboured by our fellow citizens so many miles away.

Rugged Albertans want to feel they control their own destiny.

But they watch in dismay as important business decisions are made in Toronto (while major national government decisions are made even further away in Ottawa or Hull, Quebec).

For those of us who live much closer to Toronto, the fact that this city has such an overbearing impact on our lives is no easier to bear.

Just when you thought you were getting ahead, just when you were learning how to succeed in the corporate world, Toronto

Big Banks or Toronto Big Business has again shoved you aside, sucked the joy out of your life and shaken your confidence in the future.

Look out. Here comes Toronto with your latest marching orders.

Fun time is over. Follow the new rules.

Give up some family time. Get working even harder – or get out of the way.

The Toronto Business culture is taking over. Hey everyone: TGIM – Thank God It's Monday!

And future generations may be getting groomed for life in the rat race. In a series of excellent, thought-provoking articles, The Toronto Star's Andrea Gordon noted children are under pressure to mature fast and adopt the structures of an adult world they can ill afford to live in. As Gordon notes:

> "Roderic Beaujot, sociology professor at the University of Western Ontario, revealed that today's youth are experiencing the longest-ever adolescence... Beaujot's study, Delayed Life Transitions: Trends and Implications, found that over the past 40 years, Canadians have staged a revolution in life-course patterns. They are taking longer to finish school, leave home, start full-time work, marry and have children. In 2001, 41 per cent of those age 20 to 29 were living with their parents, while 20 years earlier, only 28 per cent were still at home... Peggy Nash, 52,... has two sons living at home, Colin, 25, and Thomas, 18. Colin went to university in Guelph for four years and is back home and paying a bargain rent while he works to pay off student loans. Nash... left her own parents' home when she was 21. But lack of affordable housing, especially in urban centres, makes it much harder for youth than it used to be. And the result is a delayed transition to independence for many young adults." 6.

Again, the dilemma being described isn't unique to Toronto. But it seems to be most inflamed in Toronto where sky-high real estate costs and expensive rent leaves far too many people living in their parents' basements not be choice but by necessity.

I also believe that Toronto's overly hyper success-oriented, competitive culture raises such high expectations for new generations that these standards can never be achieved, leaving many youth, demoralized and adrift in a sea of failure, real and perceived. Toronto, perhaps more than anywhere else, pushes its youth into an organized, semi-corporate life.

But Gordon notes that it can be difficult breaking free of any strict regimen, even if it's self-imposed. She observes:

> "These days, when the biggest shortage that plagues most middle-class families is time, taking steps to get more of it seems so difficult. Trying to leap off the merry-go-round is a lot harder than it sounds once you're on it... The streaming starts early. Kids who show an aptitude in anything - art, gymnastics, violin, academics - are encouraged early to jump to the next level, which demands more time and money. Parents are reluctant to hold them back... Alvin Rosenfeld, co-author of The Over-scheduled Child: Avoiding the Hyper-parenting Trap, urges parents to consider an opposite approach to much of the conventional wisdom they may hear. Resist pressure to push your child to excel early. Focus on yourself and your spouse, because children do better when their parents are happy. Build lots of empty spaces into the calendar. Spend time together to teach children that performance and constant activity aren't the defining measures of a fulfilling life." [7]

Gordon notes that while organized sports and lessons have become a trademark of middle-class childhood, it's the freewheeling stuff that most child development experts, psychologists and educators yearn to see. They say spontaneous play, whether alone, in a playground or lying on a bedroom floor, is the breeding ground for imagination and creativity. As Gordon notes:

> "The limited free time they do have is increasingly devoted to passive activities like video and computer games or television, which have become staples of the modern home... But in the quest to develop well-rounded citizens prepared to handle whatever the future throws at them, adults have created a situation in which free play time appears to have gone the way of the pogo stick. The paradox is that in depriving kids of spontaneous play, we short-change them by not giving them the opportunity to develop creativity that will help them compete as adults... Over the years, theorists determined that free play that calls upon a child's imagination is critical in the development of both their minds and bodies - for everything from motor skills to conflict resolution." [8.]

But it seems we can't wait to turn our children into young adults and plop them on the same work world treadmill we're on. Again, although this situation isn't unique to Toronto, this fast-paced city has perhaps a more exaggerated version of the tendency to groom kids for success – childhood be damned.

Gordon points out that society expects much more from children at younger ages. She notes that "day camp used to mean splashing in wading pools, hours weaving plastic gimp bracelets and many rounds of "If You're Happy and You Know It." But this summer, one Toronto organization is offering a university preparatory camp for high school grads to "give your child the edge" in the fall… Stress and anxiety are becoming so prevalent that mental health organizations like Youth Net are going into classrooms to raise awareness among high school students. Kids aren't the only ones feeling it. Many parents going full-tilt to give their children every opportunity are feeling overwhelmed." 9.

Gordon asks: "What are we doing to our children? To ourselves? Is this the kind of family life we always wanted? Dashing from one place to the next. The constant raising of the academic bar. Exhausted parents. Stressed-out kids. No time for free play... Or even to pursue a spiritual life. Children so wired on virtual entertainment, junk food and a packed agenda that they're incapable of making their own fun? 10.

. It seems to be a recipe for giving children the same stress-related ills afflicting many adults. As Gordon notes:

"Canadian journalist Carl Honore is somewhat of an expert when it comes to slowing down. His new book, In Praise Of Slow, examines the new so-called "slow movements" taking place around the world in response to speed-obsessed society. "Children are not born obsessed with speed and productivity - we make them that way," Honore writes in his chapter on raising unhurried kids… It's something that Michelle Irwin of Markham has always guarded against with her two children, Matt, 18, and Samantha, 14. She knows first-hand the risks of driving kids too hard. A self-described Type A personality, Irwin got herself so stressed out as a teen that she ended up in hospital. As a result, she and her husband decided early to limit the kids to one outside activity at a time... Irwin says the pressure to hurry children is everywhere. At their co-op preschool, she listened to parents clamour for phonics and math for their 3-year-olds. She has worked in public schools and seen many kids exhausted by their schedules." 11.

Gordon adds that: "The pressure to excel academically is fierce. Coming just behind the double cohort, they still face a situation of too many university applicants for too few spaces. They need good marks and must be well-rounded by pursuing extra-curricular and volunteer work. They hold down part-time jobs. [12.]

"The parents are worried, so the children are hurried," Gordon asserts, adding:

"When fear sets in, it's natural to try to exert control - wherever possible. So amid a societal mantra that we are failing to keep up, and fresh memories of corporate downsizing and the collapse of the dot-com boom, that's what many parents are trying to do. They do whatever it takes to give their own children a leg up... They've done it by demanding tougher schools, a heftier curriculum and standardized testing to measure performance. Outside the school system, they fill in the gaps with tutoring, music lessons, art classes, gymnastics and hockey. For those who can't afford it, there's the additional stress and fear that their kids don't stand a chance... David Elkind, renowned child psychologist and author of The Hurried Child, says hyper-parenting is a reaction to a world changing so fast we have no idea how to prepare kids for it. Parents can't envision the society their kids will inhabit as adults, so they try to cover all the possibilities, cramming in as much as possible and operating on the principle that earlier is better." [13.]

Unfortunately, in an effort to make children successful adults, parents in Toronto and elsewhere may instead be sowing the seeds for future failure by setting the bar too high and taking the fun out of life. After all, there's plenty of time to experience the drudgery of an office job.

Reporter: "Mel, isn't this a little self-serving and egotistical naming this square after yourself?"
Mel Lastman: "Yes."
Interview exchange during the opening of Mel Lastman Square.

"I find it simply amazing that so many of you look just like your mayor - Mel Lastman."

Dame Edna - (female impersonator Barry Humphries) looking out over a packed audience during a performance in Toronto. The comical remark came at the height of the controversy over Mel Lastman fathering a former mistress's children during a lengthy extramarital affair.

"Black, who sold his interest in the Post in 2001, has long been considered by many to be little more than a pompous blowhard - a sort of Mel Lastman in noble refinery."

Linda McQuaig, Toronto writer, offering the ultimate putdown of media baron Conrad Black by comparing him to Mel Lastman.

5

The Last Man You'd Want For Mayor

Mel Lastman is truly the last man you'd think anyone would want as mayor. His public gaffes were so numerous and moronic that you'd think he'd have trouble getting elected to a small town council.

Yet this short, annoying, grand-standing politician was Toronto's mayor for years.

And Toronto is still trying to recover from its years under the bombastic Lastman.

Lastman was the former mayor of the former North York before it merged along with other former Metro Toronto municipalities to become the new City of Toronto, population 2.5 million (the Greater Toronto Area is 5 million).

Lastman was also the president of the Bad Boy furniture store chain and is best known for coming up with the witless line: "Who's better than Bad Boy? Nooooobody." My, how droll.

Incredibly, he beat out far more competent opponents to become mayor of the expanded City of Toronto.

Within months of taking office in the late 1990s, Lastman was making embarrassing mis-statements and committing one public gaffe after another.

For example, in 1999, a large winter snowfall, prompted Lastman to declare Toronto in a state of emergency and call in the army to help clear Toronto's sidewalks and streets.

Toronto had received no more snow than many other Ontario communities that did not call in the army. Lastman's over-blown reaction to a fully expected winter snowfall made the city the laughing stock of Canada for months.

Many suggested that when the snow melted, Lastman would panic again and call in the navy.

Things took another bizarre turn when reporter Adam Vaughan received death threats from Lastman after Vaughn reported on Lastman's wife Marilyn's involvement in a shoplifting incident.

And, Lastman declared war on "squeegee kids," taking aim at impoverished people whose only source of income is from donations received while cleaning vehicle windows.

Yet whenever anyone asked questions about his shoplifting wife, his treatment of those who might be his illegitimate children, or his "off the cuff" comments, Lastman would become enraged and make even more embarrassing statements.

Then, most incredibly, Lastman was re-elected in November 2000 to a second term with something like an 80 per cent approval rating. At this point, national hatred for Toronto was joined by bewilderment and pity.

Just days after his second-term victory, Lastman shocked the public once again by admitting to a long-term affair with a former employee, Grace Louie. Her adult sons, Kim and Todd Louie, brought Lastman to court in a highly publicized paternity suit.

Lastman stunned the entire nation when he sheepishly admitted to a longstanding affair with Louie while he was in the Bad Boy furniture business, before he got into politics but while married to his current wife Marilyn, mother of his three sons.

He said he was owning up about the affair because he'd learned that Louie was filing lawsuits seeking support.

After repeatedly embarrassing himself and Toronto, Lastman was at it again, acknowledging a 14-year affair with a married woman that ended in 1971, before he became mayor of North York.

Lastman, a 30-year political veteran, has neither confirmed nor denied fathering Louie's sons.

But he has admitted to paying Louie $27,500 back in 1974 as a one-time only payment in exchange for her silence about the affair.

Louie and her sons – both were in their 40s – were seeking $4.5 million in retroactive child support.

But in May 2001, the Ontario Superior Court struck down the Louies' attempt to proceed with civil action against Lastman.

Subsequently, Louie and her two grown sons ultimately lost their bid to appeal the court decision that dismissed their attempts to seek child support from Mayor Mel Lastman.

Louie and her sons Kim and Todd had simply waited far too long to launch civil actions against Lastman, ruled Justice Marc Rosenberg of the Ontario Court of Appeal: "The 30-year delay in bringing the claim after the affair ended was fatal to its success," he wrote, adding, "the appellant knew all of the facts giving rise to the claim either in 1971 when the affair ended or at the latest in 1980, when the youngest child turned 18. Any possible claim she had could have been brought then."

That the short and unattractive Lastman could have carried on a long-standing affair soon became the butt of jokes. Comics suggested the diminutive Lastman initially felt so good about the affair he felt 5-feet-tall.

Dame Edna Everage (female impersonator Barry Humphries) also weighed in on the embarrassing scandal.

At a sold-out appearance in Toronto, Australia's Dame Edna made reference to the scandal and Lastman's proclivity for fathering illegitimate children out of wedlock.

Dame Edna remarked to the entire audience that: "It's amazing how much all of you look like your mayor - Mel Lastman."

By 2002 however, the joke was wearing thin and his approval ratings had sunk so low, that Toronto's tiny imperfect mayor did not seek another term, when his second term expired in November 2003.

While in office however, he did an enormous amount of damage to Toronto's reputation and may have single-handedly increased the numbers of people – not just in Canada, but around the world – who hate Toronto.

Former Toronto Mayor Mel Lastman is so reviled; his name has become a sort of shorthand for putting down anyone considered guilty of inept show-boating.

For example, Toronto author Linda McQuaig recently offered the ultimate putdown of media baron Conrad Black by comparing him in an unflattering light to Mel Lastman: "Black, who sold his interest in the Post in 2001, has long been considered by many to be little more than a pompous blowhard – a sort of Mel Lastman in noble refinery." [1]

Mayor Mel Lastman shamelessly mugged for the camera and fawned over American real estate tycoon Donald Trump in 2001 when Trump announced his intentions to build a 65-storey Trump International Hotel & Tower, with hotel units on the first 33 floors and residential condos on the remaining 35.

Although Toronto has seen larger projects, Lastman is something of a clinging fan to foreign celebrities, whether he's sucking up to famous businessmen like Trump or embarrassing the city by virtually begging flash-in-the-pan foreign stars such as a former Spice Girl to visit Toronto.

This superficial, mindless superfan approach to politics extended into the important business community.

Lastman hit a new low in 2002 when the diminutive mayor addressed the black-tie dinner gathering of the Toronto Board of Trade with a speech that disclosed Lastman was a fan of the business community – and that was about the extent of meaningful content in his rambling address.

Putting this as charitably as possible, the speech was short on substance and long on stupidity.

Lastman "treated" the distinguished gathering with tired and tasteless one-liners.

The unimpressed black tie audience of more than 2,000 prominent business executives was enraged by the complete lack of any informative or insightful content in Lastman's meandering, semi-coherent "speech."

It was another squandered opportunity, another embarrassing escapade from a former mayor who served up plenty of both during his time in office.

In a biting editorial following Lastman's business speech bungle, the normally Lastman-supportive Toronto Star declared that: "Lastman's antics are wearing thin," while asserting that the business gathering deserved more than off-colour wisecracks and "stream-of-consciousness musings about a weak dollar and his own political woes."

The editorial charged that: "His Worship cannot be trusted to handle even the routine duties of office responsibly," before concluding that the mayor should get his act together fast or immediately resign.

But Lastman wasn't about to do either.

The man who often said the only thing he feared in politics was his own mouth, managed to shove his foot in his gum-flapping pie-hole yet again.

And this gaffe would prove very costly to Toronto and all of Canada.

In June 2002, news broke that the mystifying mayor had jokingly told a reporter he was worried about being boiled in a big pot by cannibals in Mombassa.

The remark came shortly before he was to visit the African nation of Kenya.

"Why the hell would I want to go to a place like Mombassa?" the short, perpetually self-destructive mayor told a freelance journalist. "I just see myself in a pot of boiling water with all these natives dancing around me."

Lastman was inexplicably uttering racist remarks during an event that was intended to help promote Toronto's bid for the 2008 Olympics.

And he made his moronic, clown-like, cannibals comment just weeks before the vote was to take place to decide whether the Games would be held in Toronto or someplace else.

News of Lastman's stupid and offensive – not to mention unfunny – comment came virtually on the eve of the International Olympics Committee making its decision on the 2008 host city.

And five of the voting judges were from various African nations.

The OIC vice-president was an African-American who was not amused by Mel's "joke," stating it's indicative of how the mayor thinks (that's actually a kind response considering many people wonder *if* he thinks).

That's half-a-dozen votes Lastman threw away, half-a-dozen votes that could have made a difference in the city selection vote outcome.

International headlines erupted overnight, with many news reports questioning how Toronto can put itself forward as a city welcoming of all nationalities to one of the most ethnically diverse communities in the world.

One wag dubbed the diminutive mayor a "tiny tanned time bomb" with a world view "shaped in equal parts by Tarzan movies and Bugs Bunny cartoons."

It was another stunning, staggering and humiliating embarrassment for Toronto.

It was also a very demoralizing disappointment for the thousands of Canadian volunteers that helped with Toronto's bid.

Toronto ended up losing the Games to Beijing.

Although it was reported that Lastman's asinine remark did not cost Toronto – and Canada – the Games, I have a hard time believing that.

All of Canada had been cheering for Toronto in hopes the Games would be held in Canada.

While Lastman alone was to blame for his offensive remark, many blamed Toronto for letting the entire nation down.

If that seems a little harsh or unfair, consider that Toronto citizens willingly voted into their mayoralty job, this Clown Prince of Politics. Twice.

Just months later, Mel messed up again. Once again, he simply lost his mind and didn't know where to find it.

Lastman's popularity began dropping like a stone in the polls after he shook hands with a member of the Hells Angels biker gang during a highly publicized gathering of the group in downtown Toronto in 2002.

On hearing that the notorious biker gang was meeting in Toronto, Lastman went out of his way to meet them, leaving his home to travel across the city to meet them.

Once again, it was time for Superfan Mel to fawn over the famous.

And on arriving at the meeting, Lastman wasted no time in introducing himself as the mayor of Toronto to a burly biker who extended his hand.

The biker and the mayor then shook hands as camera flash bulbs erupted in a lightning storm.

As always, it was some time before Mel realized he'd done something wrong. Again.

Laurie Monsebraaten of The Toronto Star had this report on the controversial handshake and Lastman's other self-inflicted woes:

"A photo of the handshake caused national outrage when it ran in a local newspaper. The handshake also drew ire from communities like Montreal that are fighting to rid themselves of the criminal organization.

The biker gang, notorious for drug dealing and prostitution, has been linked to more than a hundred killings in Quebec.

Toronto police are concerned the group will cause similar problems here, if its recent growth in Ontario isn't checked.

Many local officers also said the mayor's glad-handing photo was a slap in the face. However, Lastman, who said "curiosity" drove him to visit the biker convention, claimed he didn't know the extent of the gang's criminal activity...

Since his re-election Lastman has been dogged by an embarrassing paternity suit, international ridicule on the Olympic stage and political sniping at city hall... Last summer, the city auditor released a scathing report on the city's finance department, noting the absence of rudimentary accounting procedures had lead to millions of dollars worth of questionable consulting contracts... serious irregularities in a computer leasing deal with MFP Financial Services Ltd. of Mississauga..." 2.

As if to add insult to injury, Lastman then held a press conference where he refused to answer questions about why he was worried African cannibals would make soup out of him.

He then monotoned the same wooden apology, stating he was sorry, more than 20 times: "I am truly sorry I made the remarks. My comments were inappropriate. I'm very sorry. I should not have made those comments. I'm sorry. It was the wrong thing to say. I'm sorry. I'm sorry."

It's Miller Time

Within weeks of taking office, Toronto Mayor David Miller had proven to be a far more competent and effective mayor than his predecessor. Not that it's a difficult achievement. It's almost like damning with faint praise.

In fact, Miller's mayoralty term has so far been so competent and efficient that there's really very little to criticize, a fact that drove Toronto Star humour columnist Linwood Barclay to distraction. Venting his frustration, Barclay explained: "I can't begin to tell you how disappointed I've been with Mayor Miller. From the moment he was elected, he's managed to put one foot in front of the other, instead of in his mouth. When he's opened that, coherent words and phrases have come forth, he has, more or less, managed to deliver on the things he said he would deliver on... In short, David Miller has failed to be an embarrassment. Since he's taken office, I have not done one column making fun of him..." 3.

Barclay notes Miller did manage to make one gaffe: In a private conversation with another Ontario mayor, he jokingly asked how thing's were with his counterpart's police force - because most of Toronto's cops were in jail. The light-hearted remark referring to scandals plaguing the Toronto force was picked up by the media and Miller was forced to apologize.

Still, it left Barclay little to go on: "Okay, so it was a dumb comment for a mayor to make. But for me, it lacked the punch of say, joking that you're afraid to go to Africa because you'll be tossed into a big pot by cannibals, or shaking hands with the visiting hells Angels delegation, or going on CNN and admitting for all the world to see, that you've never even heard of something called the World Health Organization... It is frankly, pretty disappointing. But it is a start. And for the moment, it's all that people like me, working in the Cheap Shot Dept., have got. And that's why I'm willing to hold off on calling for David Miller's resignation. But if he doesn't say something else stupid soon - I'm going to give him until the end of the month - then the gloves are off." 4.

Toronto Star columnist Royson James accompanied Miller during a visit to New York City and found the mayor was a tireless promoter of all things Toronto, effectively conveying the city's strengths to business audiences and influential publications throughout Manhattan.

In response, New York Deputy Mayor Daniel Doctoroff lauded Toronto as one of the great cities of the world with a great deal of synergy with NYC and many similarities, including waterfront land opportunities, and status as the economic and creative centre of our respective nations. 5.

The next day had Miller delivering a strong speech before a gathering of 100 business leaders in Manhattan. Miller told the gathering that Toronto is the most cost-competitive large city in the world, is home to nearly all of the biggest legal and accounting firms in Canada and the nation's leading centre of commerce - poised for an unprecedented growth cycle that has created a palpable air of excitement and enthusiasm.

James notes: "Massive development projects, including $1.5-billion in university, health and research facilities, and Donald Trump's $500-million hotel and residential tower combine with a cultural renaissance sparked by new or renovated buildings for opera, museum and art." 6.

In Miller's own words: "The salient aspect of doing business with Toronto is that you get more for less... Torontonians are feeling bold. They know how great their city is, and they are hungry to share it with the rest of the world... ours is a city that is buzzing with energy... We have to believe that our city can be spectacular in ways that no one has yet imagined. We have to be unabashedly passionate and visionary in our ideas. For Toronto, 'good enough' simply is not good enough." 7.

Miller is definitely a welcome change from Lastman. Miller is much more competent - although how hard would it be to outshine Lastman? Again, it almost amounts to damning with faint praise.

But Miller also goes too far at times, displaying the condescending Toronto arrogance that so many people find annoying. A case in point: Miller's Lastman-like assumption that because Toronto is the nation's biggest city, that means it deserves some sort of special city-state-like status and the right to meet on an equal footing with senior levels of government.

That not everyone agrees with Mayor Miller's viewpoint clearly doesn't sit well with His Worship, who has made his disgust known.

Toronto's self-centred and selfish attitude is more than merely annoying. It's also harmful to other urban centres, perhaps even harmful to Toronto itself. The Toronto Star's Joseph Hall explained the issue in report noting it's just as expensive to build a bridge or fix a road in Dufferin County as it is in Toronto. [8]

Hall's report quoted a number of municipal leaders who are alarmed by Toronto's opposition to upper level government funding being spread around on a per capita basis, instead of going chiefly to Toronto alone. [9]

Noting that needed repairs to town and county infrastructure have been put off due to the county's meagre tax base, Dufferin warden Keith Thompson takes "great issue with the argument that Toronto needs the money more than we do," and says that if municipalities outside of Toronto cannot function properly due to lack of funding, this situation will ultimately impact on Toronto as well. [10]

"The people who run Toronto somehow can't see that in the music business and the entertainment business there are no more than four, possibly five, venues in the entire world that are synonymous with the birth of rock 'n' roll. Madison Square Garden is one. The Hollywood Bowl is probably another. The Glasgow Apollo is another. And Maple Leaf Gardens is the other. I think there should be a plaque put up that says: This famous building full of heritage and history was turned into a grocery store by the wankers who call themselves politicians for Toronto. Because one day – probably long after I'm dead and buried – the city will come to regret it."

Rick Wakeman, legendary keyboardist for the English progressive rock band *Yes,* reflecting on the decision to turn Maple Leaf Gardens into a grocery store.

"The Air Canada Centre has a capacity of 19,500 people, yet only about 1,500 of the seats go on sale to the public after season-ticket holders have gobbled up the rest. It wouldn't be as disappointing if these season-ticket holders were big hockey fans, but most of them wear suits and spend the game discussing mergers and stocks. To add insult to injury, the 'suits' often don't show up until halfway through the period, if at all."

Heather Manley, hockey fan, reflecting on ordinary fans getting frozen out of hockey rinks by Big Business.

6

Spoiled Sports

Toronto is a major league sports town filled with rabid fans – none of them able to afford the ridiculously steep ticket prices charged to attend home games at the SkyDome, the old Maple Leaf Gardens or, now, since the dawn of new millennium, the Air Canada Centre.

Of course, that's if they can even get tickets. Hockey fan Heather Manley summed up the frustration of many when she wrote a letter to the Toronto Star complaining:

"Leafs fans just don't have a chance! There's almost no better feeling for a real Leafs fan than attending a live game and watching the Buds play in front of a home crowd. Unfortunately, it's a feeling that only a select few in Ontario get to experience. The Air Canada Centre has a capacity of 19,500 people, yet only about 1,500 of the seats go on sale to the public after season-ticket holders have gobbled up the rest. It wouldn't be as disappointing if these season-ticket holders were big hockey fans, but most of them wear suits and spend the game discussing mergers and stocks. To add insult to injury, the 'suits' often don't show up until halfway through the period, if at all. Compare that to 'Joe Nobody' stuck in the back of the standing-room-only section, ripping the stitches in his Leafs jersey as he stretches to see past the large support pillar that obstructs his view… Ordinary fans have no choice but to duke it out on Ticketmaster or ebay to have any chance of securing a nosebleed seat for a post-season game…" [1].

And that nosebleed seat with an obstructed view can be expensive. Very expensive.

Indeed, a road trip game can be cheaper than a local match played at the ACC. In a Toronto Star article cleverly titled 'Road trip cheaper than ACC', numerous Toronto Maple Leafs fans bemoaned the high cost of tickets that are well beyond the reach of most ordinary people.

Some of these fans had travelled to Buffalo in early April 2004 to see the Leafs beat the Sabres 2-0 and avoid being eliminated in the playoffs.

A Grand Game

The group then travelled to Ottawa to watch them beat the Senators in early playoff action. Even with the exchange rate taken into account, that entire weekend in Buffalo and Ottawa was less than half the cost of seeing the Leafs play on home ice the following week in Game 2 against the Senators.

A pair of good Leafs-Sens tickets at the ACC could set you back as much as $900 to $1,000 assuming you could get a pair of tickets at all, even from scalpers. [2].

It's not just that the Leafs finally had a respectable shot at the Stanley Cup after 36 Stanley Cupless years. No, that wasn't the key reason for the overpriced and scarce tickets.

The big reason is that Corporate Canada – make that Corporate Toronto (same thing, come to think of it) – routinely buys up the best seats at inflated prices so companies can hand them out as baubles and bribes to sales reps, customers, the chosen few.

This corporate screening "accomplishes" two things: It serves to keep ticket prices artificially high while also keeping the average fans – the riff raff – well removed from the choice seats.

If not for such civic-minded corporations, the Leafs might have to sell tickets at affordable prices and real families might get to see live sports action up close.

But thanks to the timely intervention of these faceless, heartless, soulless, upstanding corporate citizens, actual fans of the game are relegated to over-priced seats high in the stands where they can think themselves lucky that they can afford any seats at all.

Fans Frozen Off Ice

A few real fans may glance wistfully at the vacant choice seats left empty by uncaring corporations that are often lax in handing out these perks to VIPs (Very Important Persons – not Condescending Undeserving Elitists, as that acronym would be CUE).

Toronto is ruled by corporations and these corporations have decreed the little people may still watch the game, but preferably far away. Perhaps on TV. In Barrie.

Overheard conversation:

Man: "Honey, I think I can snag us a pair of Leafs tickets for just two-weeks take-home pay."

Woman: "Are you forgetting our combined pay isn't enough to pay the rent – on the basement apartment in my parents' house? Last time we were late, dad broke our legs and it took forever to get to the food bank to pick up our groceries…"

Two-weeks pay for a pair of sports tickets is really quite reasonable. In Russia.

Of course sky-high ticket prices are only one component of the Toronto sports/entertainment experience.

Keeping with our Toronto-Moscow comparison, parking is also reasonable – some rates are less than a day's pay – and choice spots are available less than two miles from the sports venue. After your 1.9-mile trek in the rain, the fully enclosed venue will protect you from the weather – until the game's over. Don't worry, you'll find your car. Just keep walking. And walking. And walking…

Food is also surprisingly affordable. With interest rates at historic lows, easy payment plans can be arranged for a hamburger, cardboard-flavoured fries and watery beer. For a modest added premium, make it a cheeseburger.

Overheard conversation:

Same man: "Honey, I found an amazing deal – pair of tickets, parking, two hotdogs and a beer with a couple of straws, all for just twelve-hundred bucks…"

Different woman: "Great – but shouldn't you discuss this with your wife?"

The prices are sky high, whether the sports event is at the ACC or the old Maple Leaf gardens.

Speaking of Maple Leaf Gardens, Toronto is intent on turning this legendary, venerable edifice into a… wait for it… grocery store. I kid you not.

Wakeman Whacks Wankers

And, gentle reader, you and I are not the only ones stunned by this bizarre turn of events.

Rick Wakeman, legendary keyboardist for the English progressive rock band Yes, told CREEM magazine in June, 2004:

"I think there should be a plaque put up that says: This famous building full of heritage and history was turned into a grocery store by the wankers who call themselves politicians for Toronto. Because one day – probably long after I'm dead and buried – the city will come to regret it." Incidentally, "wankers" is an English term for people who are regularly seduced, physically pleasured and satisfied by one of their own hands.

Beyond some of the greatest hockey games ever played (the impressive structure has been dark since the Toronto Maple Leafs played their first game at the ACC in 1999), Maple Leaf Gardens was the site of the famous boxing matches, including the historic Mohamed Ali versus George Chuvalo match, political conventions and special events.

"Politicians should be Shot"

Maple Leaf gardens was also home to some truly legendary concerts by the Yes, the Beatles, the Who, Three Dog Night, Bob Dylan, The Guess Who, Neil Young, Rush, Frank Sinatra, The Rolling Stones, Alice Cooper and Elvis Presley to name only a very few. Now it's being turned into a Loblaws supermarket and the only ice will be in the frozen foods section.

Stating the decision to turn this remarkable entertainment venue into a common grocery store simply "stuns me," Wakeman adds that Toronto politicians "should be shot" for failing to protect or even recognize a priceless diamond when they see one: "The people who run Toronto somehow can't see that in the music business and the entertainment business there are no more than four, possibly five, venues in the entire world that are synonymous with the birth of rock 'n' roll. Madison Square Garden is one. The Hollywood Bowl is probably another. The Glasgow Apollo is another. And Maple Leaf Gardens is the other."

Another plea for sanity was heard from the United States. In a letter to the Toronto Star, Tony Fusco, president of the Art

Deco Society of Boston, Mass., praised Maple Leaf Gardens: "Architecturally, the building is a masterful combination of art deco and Streamlined Moderne detailing rarely seen in any country. As such, any re-use that does not respect its architectural integrity, both exterior and interior, would be a major loss." 3.

Noting this opinion is shared by art deco architectural experts in Toronto, across Canada and throughout the world, Fusco stresses the interior's importance will be forever lost as a public venue, gathering place and hockey arena if the supermarket proposal were to proceed. He adds: "It is our view that the best outcome for this building would be one that fundamentally preserves the interior space for future generations... You have an opportunity to make an important statement about the value of your heritage to all your citizens and to the world." 4.

Unfortunately, such pleas have fallen on deaf ears. Toronto City Council wasn't paying any heed to words of wisdom from Canada, England, the United States or anywhere else in the world.

Gardens Salad for Grocery Aisles

In late June 2004, City Council gave approval to convert the Carlton Street shrine into a grocery store.

It was another sad example of Toronto taking its heritage, architecture and traditions for granted.

Soon, Maple Leaf Gardens will literally be a shell of its former self. The building's imposing monolithic exterior will still stand. But its heart and guts will be ripped out.

Anyone hunting for hockey heroes will instead find hot dog buns and TV dinners.

An important part of Toronto and Canadian culture is being discarded for no good reason. Once again, Toronto is callously squandering something wonderful.

I come from Hamilton where the only pro sports team is the Canadian Football League Hamilton Tiger-Cats.

For the most part, this CFL team is well supported by the citizenry and most games are well attended despite Hamilton's population being but one-tenth of Greater Toronto's.

In contrast, Toronto has the CFL Argonauts, Hamilton's historic rival. Toronto's deep pockets ensure the Argos are laden with many of the most talented players available, players Hamilton can ill afford to acquire.

Hamilton is by comparison a modest, honest industrial city with an old, open-air stadium, in sharp contrast, again, to Toronto's Skydome, a state-of-the-art sports complex with a re-tractable roof.

Skydome Not Good Enough For Toronto

Incredible as it may seem to anyone outside Toronto, Torontonians now look on Skydome as an antiquated dud that's hardly worth their time.

Despite the city's enormous population, there's also a lack of fervent support for the Argos, a team that normally performs well but rarely draws a sold-out audience for home games. Torontonians take the Argos for granted – and some dream of an NFL team, they'd also likely ignore.

And this somewhat fickle fan base can also be somewhat ambivalent when it comes to some of Toronto's other pro teams, which include the NBA basketball team Toronto Raptors, the AL major league baseball team the Toronto Blue Jays – two-time World Series champions – and the aforementioned NHL Maple Leafs.

There are also pro or semi-pro soccer and lacrosse teams. That's big league baseball, football, hockey, soccer, lacrosse and basketball… just about any sport you can think of, a plethora of entertaining sports sources for Toronto's spoiled fan base.

And there's the Hockey Hall of Fame, a remarkable at-traction unrivalled anywhere in the world. As I wrote in a feature story on the hall, it's an interactive paradise. I wrote:

"Visit the Hockey Hall of Fame and you'll get can get a chance to go one-on-one against the Toronto Maple Leafs goalie - or at least a life-sized digital version of him. Picture yourself or a family member gripping a hockey stick and taking a hard shot, sending an orange puck flying, while Balfour - one of the top-ranked goalies in the NHL - lunges to make the save. This interactive game is in the NHLPA Be A Player Zone, focal point of the newly renovated North Concourse. The Zone features an expanded faux-ice rink surface and scoreboard to register your goals. It replaces an earlier interactive version about half the size and operating with less sophisticated technology. Bob Stellick, spokesman for the Hockey Hall of Fame, says the introduction of Balfour as goalie, combined with technological advancements, help make this interactive game "very realistic and exciting." If you're more of a net minder, you can test your mettle in an interactive game against Wayne Gretzky or Mark Messier. Or you can play the role of announcer. With a new gondola feature overlooking the Zone, visitors will take a hands-on approach to hockey broadcasting. You'll also want to check out the virtual Hockey Broadcast Museum, which enables visitors to go deep into the history of broadcast media. You can also test your hockey knowledge via the Pepsi Game Time trivia game... June 18 is the 10th anniversary of the relocation of the Hockey Hall of Fame - founded in 1943 - to BCE Place at Yonge and Front." [5.]

In contrast, Hamilton – also a major city, though smaller than Toronto – has but one pro team, the CFL Tiger Cats and its sports shrine is the Canadian Football Hall of Fame, a nice facility, but no pigskin palace can ever be as big a draw as Toronto's

Hockey hall in a country where hockey rules. But if Hamilton feels short-changed, you can only imagine how other Canadian cities must feel.

Just consider that most Canadian cities have no pro sports teams at all (and would cheerfully kill to have even one), and you can begin to understand the resentment towards a city that often treats its rich sports and cultural traditions with a degree of ambivalence that sometimes borders on indifference. To some extent, this indifference is more perception than reality as many true-blue fans can't afford – or even find – tickets to support these major league teams. Many of the empty seats we see belong to millionaire businessmen who can't be bothered to attend.

Even so, perceptions and impressions are powerful things, and for cities with no pro teams of their own, Toronto's seeming disregard for its overflowing sports platter is difficult to stomach.

Entertainment Events Also Taken For Granted

Toronto also takes major entertainment events for granted. Most Canadian cities would love to host the Juno Awards – Hamilton certainly loved playing host for several years and Edmonton drew 10,000 boisterous music fans.
But as pop music critic Ben Rayner reported in The Toronto Star, Canada's major music awards event didn't meet with anything approaching Edmonton's frenzy when the event was held in "blasé Toronto." 6.

Perhaps Toronto thinks it can take such a callous approach without any repercussions. Certainly Toronto is a magnet for talent. The Toronto Star routinely devotes a two-page spread to photos of major movies stars and rock star and sports figures in town. Yet this also serves as a reminder to non-Torontonians the city is so awash in stars it can fill inside pages with them. But it's rarely front page news…

"Never once while I was growing up (in Toronto) did it ever occur to me that I could be struck in the spine by a bullet while standing in line to get a sandwich. Fortunately, I was able to escape to rural Ontario before my native city was completely overrun by violent crime."
Mark Hoult, former Torontonian commenting on shootings.

"It's too large now. And there's too much crime and too many killings."
Linda Puder, survey participant, Hamilton.

"There's also too many gangs and crime going on there. It's not safe to walk the streets in Toronto."
Gene Mason, survey participant, Hamilton.

"I also hate the violence there, the street gangs."
Wendy Sibley, survey participant, Hamilton.

"Toronto can be quite disgusting sometimes. It's one of the few places where people will urinate and pleasure themselves on the street. It's a violent city also."
Laura Wysocki, survey participant, Cambridge, Ontario.

7

Toronto the Good, the Bad & the Ugly

Toronto The Good – as it likes to be known – is a crime riddled city. The last time I did a weekend guest reporter stint for The Toronto Star; there were four murders that Saturday. All of them involved black victims and gunmen in violent neighbourhoods.

Nor is murder purely a weekend pastime. On a random day in May, I glanced at the Star's GTA section and found three homicides on a Tuesday. (Senior fatally beaten at nursing home, B2; Family desperate to find killer, B3; and Man, 44, found dead, B3, Toronto Star, Wednesday, May 26, 2004).

What's most disturbing about all three murders – two of them with senior citizen victims – is that each was committed by non-family members.

The significance is this: You can often try and reassure yourself that you enjoy a fair bit of security and protection from society's darker elements when you consider statistics that indicate most homicides are the result of one family member killing another. If you're not a member of a violent family, you're safe, you think. But when strangers take the lives of citizens through crimes of opportunity and convenience or random acts of violence, then, as a society, you've really got serious problems.

Nor can you realistically take comfort in the fact that Toronto's violent crime rate is miniscule compared to American cities the same size.

U.S. Comparison Meaningless

Only Americans think America is normal. In truth, the U.S. is an anomaly in the civilized world. Its insane, murder-friendly gun laws have made it a country at war from within.

U.S. violent crime rates are far higher than those in Canada, true. They're also far higher than those in Australia, New Zealand, England, Scotland, France, Germany, Holland, Denmark, Sweden – just about any European nation you can think of, even war-torn Northern Ireland.

No, forget the U.S. Focus instead on the fact that Toronto is seeing a growing number of homicides and the killings are being cited as a reason many people dislike, even hate, a city some see as an impersonal, dangerous metropolis.

And it's not just murders you have to worry about. Violent crime of all kinds is a concern. It's become difficult to feel safe. Witness the case of a 9-year-old Toronto girl who vanished in the middle of a birthday party. She turned up more than an hour later after being severely beaten and sexually assaulted by some sicko. An extensive police search of the area brought about the discovery of the abducted girl and the middle-aged crazy who abducted her. [1]

Commenting on spring police raids that netted a good deal of guns and drugs, Bill Dunphy, The Hamilton Spectator's foreign correspondent in Toronto, notes the Malvern neighbourhood in Toronto is "home to several gangs and hosted a quarter of this year's 19 murders – all of them involving guns and gangs." [2]

By the late 1990s, Toronto had serious problems with guns. And those problems only got worse in the new millennium. Of the 60 homicides Toronto (the city proper, not Greater Toronto, which has a population of 5-million) suffered in 2002, many were non-family members – in some cases complete strangers – lashing out in rage. In one notorious case, a gunman returned to a nightclub and shot a club staffer to death. The reason: The gunman didn't like being asked to pay a $10 cover charge. 3.

A New Breed of Killer

As The Toronto Star's Betsy Powell and Peter Small report: "Police who investigate homicides say they are dealing with a new breed of killer today. They're young, armed and can be set off over something as inconsequential as a perceived 'dis' or being searched before entering a club. Disputes once settled with fists are no finalized with guns, with lethal consequences." 4.

Indeed, consider the tragic shooting death of 17-year-old Jeffrey Reodica. Police ended up fatally shooting the youth while trying to break up a violent confrontation that rapidly escalated after one youth allegedly uttered a racial slur against another. 5.

A couple days later, police arrested a 19-year-old man in connection with the killing of Kempton Howard, a black man who was a much beloved community leader and coach.

His senseless slaying left children in his Toronto neighbourhood in tears. Howard had engaged the children in fun activities and routinely walked them safely home.

Police did not know the motive behind the killing, but it's suspected it may have been the result of an argument that escalated into something more. 6.

More arrests followed, and it appears the dedicated black volunteer worker was slain by a gang of men – most, if not all of them black – because he had asked them to stop doing drugs at the community centre. Police say it then appears an argument erupted and this quickly escalated into a vicious slaying.   7.

It seems it doesn't take much for matters to escalate into shooting deaths in Toronto.

Random, Drive-by Shootings

Sometimes it takes no provocation at all. Consider the random shooting of Louise Russo, 44, the mother of three children and primary caregiver for daughter Jenna, who was born with cerebral palsy. Russo had just ordered sandwich for her daughter at the counter of a Toronto sandwich bar when gang warfare erupted in the parking lot. One of the trigger-happy gunmen sprayed bullets recklessly into the restaurant, shooting Russo and paralysing her for life.

Hamilton Spectator correspondent Bill Dunphy notes that the horrific, senseless shooting of Russo gained little attention at first because Toronto had suffered "so many shootings, so many shattered lives… it was just more flying lead in a troubled town." 8.

Dunphy observes it wasn't until Torontonians realized that Russo was a remarkable woman providing one-to-one care for her cerebral palsy struck daughter Jenna that it was seen as something more than just another shooting – and an outpouring of sympathy and donations came pouring out. 9.

Public Desensitized to Violence

If not for Russo's compelling story of caregiver shot down for no reason, the story would have soon lost the interest of a Toronto public desensitized to the constant barrage of violent crime reports.

Toronto Star reader Mark Hoult of Havelock, Ontario is a former Torontonian who is alarmed at the way the city has changed for the worse. Commenting on the Russo shooting, Hoult raised the concern of many citizens in a letter to the editor in which he noted: "Never once while I was growing up (in Toronto) did it ever occur to me that I be struck in the spine by a bullet while standing in line to get a sandwich. Fortunately. I was able to escape to rural Ontario before my native city was completely overrun by violent crime." 10.

Predicting Toronto may see an exodus of people and businesses fleeing the city for safer communities, Hoult asks: "It rips me apart to see the city where I was born come to this – when is this going to stop?" 11.

Unfortunately, Hoult's question remains unanswered.

Shootings Happening Everywhere

The other disturbing, unfolding phenomenon about Toronto shootings is that this reckless gunplay isn't just happening in rough neighbourhoods, seedy after-hours clubs and filthy crack houses.

Shootings are happening on busy highways, in crowded shopping malls, in sandwich bars – as in Louise Russo's case – and most recently in a very posh restaurant in a swank part of town. As The Toronto Star's Shannon Proudfoot reports:

"A man is in hospital after an early morning shooting outside an upscale downtown venue that had been packed with Toronto Film Festival party-goers a few hours earlier... The victim was struck in the chin, chest and wrist and staggered to the entrance of the Rosewater Supper Club before being taken to St. Michael's hospital..." 12.

Killings that fail to show up in homicide statistics include an increasing number of suicides. These normally go unreported in the media – unless they occur in a public setting. In these cases, the suicide draws public attention that cannot be ignored. One such case occurred in June 2004 when a man brandishing a handgun on a downtown Toronto street suddenly raised the gun to his head and fired, as police and horrified bystanders looked on. 13.

Again, suicides rarely if ever show up in the crime stats. Not that these stats need any embellishing: By midyear, there were 19 unsolved murders in Toronto. 14.

Just a couple of months after Hoult's poignant letter, another random killing took place.

This time, a 36-year-old truck loader at the Ontario Food Terminal was stabbed to death at a nearby grocery store where he had stopped to pick up a coffee on his way to work.

That same morning, there were other incidents of people being knifed in the same Etobicoke area of Toronto. And there were also reports of people complaining of being followed by muggers. 15.

Streets Aren't Safe Anymore

Clearly, Toronto's streets aren't safe – for anyone. For example: In the late spring of 2004, my wife Philippa and I played host to some of her visiting relatives from England in May, 2004.

Her uncle and aunt, David and Susie Martin, wanted to explore Toronto, including a visit to the CN Tower. I dropped them off a short walk from the Tower while on my way to work an editing shift at The Toronto Star.

While at the CN Tower, David stopped off at a washroom while Susie waited outside. It was the opportunity two muggers were waiting for.

Fortunately Susie kept a tight grip on her purse and yelled loudly. The muggers fled in this case.

But how many other cases are there of tourists having their dream vacation ruined by Toronto's growing population of muggers, thugs, panhandlers and street gangs?

For a city that prides itself on being a Mecca for tourism, Toronto is fast-gaining a reputation as a city that is no longer safe.

And it seems people of all ages need to keep looking

over their shoulder. Some neighbourhoods are also home to numerous known pedophiles and sex offenders. Many are repeat offenders.

When 10-year-old Holly Jones went missing, the usual suspects – known pedophiles in the area – were questioned.

But this was a new sicko at work. Computer geek Michael Briere, 36, of Toronto, had tired of downloading child pornography and wanted the real thing.

So, he snatched the little girl off her Toronto street to fulfill his fantasy of having sex with a child.

He brutally raped Holly, then strangled her to death. Briere, who received 25 years in prison for his inhuman crime, says he raped the child and ended her life in barely 40 minutes from the time he snatched her off a city street. 16.

Repeat Sex Offenders

Even more recently, The Star ran a series of special investigative reports on Douglas Moore, a serial pedophile who became a serial killer.

As the series showed, Moore had been sexually abused by his father until his early teens when his parents divorced in 1983. He spent much of the mid-1980s sexually assaulting children.

Moore continued sexually assaulting teens in the 1990s and on into the new millennium, with most assaults, sexual and otherwise, taking place in the Greater Toronto Area. While serving prison time, he built his large frame into a muscular mass.

In late 2003, Moore killed three young men he thought had stolen money from him. He then took his own life by hanging himself. 17.

The same day The Star ran the second part of its series on Moore, another front page story noted that 7 different stabbings took place during the week, 5 of them proving fatal.

The victims were a mix of races, with blacks – who make up less than 10 per cent of Toronto's population – involved in about half the stabbings.

One of the victims pale Anglo countenance made him stand out, earning him the nickname "Whitey."

A Stabbing Every Day

As reporter Robert Cribb noted: "At least one person was stabbed each day for five consecutive days..." [18.]

And on the same day that the Star ran its story on the food terminal worker being slain, another story on the next page detailed the efforts of sex offender Martin Ferrier to return to prison.

The hulking Toronto area man, deemed an incurable psychopath, has more than 60 convictions for a range of crimes, including rape, arson, assault and forcible confinement.

He has refused all sex offender treatment in prison and has told prison doctors he wants to become Canada's most prolific killer. He was kicked out of a Mississauga motel after motel patrons discovered the chronic sex offender had checked in. [19.]

The very next day, The Star reported on an all-too-frequent occurrence: a violent situation involving a police shoot-out with an armed suspect. The story detailed a gun battle that sent a police officer and a suspect to hospital with non-life-threatening gunshot wounds. [20.]

Most of the shootings in Toronto involve black people. That's a simple statement of fact. And more often than not, the crimes amount to blacks killing other blacks, sometimes for little apparent reason other than a rude remark.

Although the statistics certainly bear out the prominence of blacks in shooting incidents, it's even apparent at a purely anecdotal level.

In March of 2004, I worked a weekend general assignment shift at The Star. And as I've mentioned, I covered four homicides in two days, all of them involving black victims and black gunmen.

To make matters more difficult to resolve, many in the predominantly black neighbourhoods where the shootings occurred were quick to blame the police for being slow to act. They were also apt to provide little information to assist police. Some seemed to be trying to shelter the killers, stating they saw and heard nothing unusual despite residing in close proximity to the crime scene.

Black-on-Black Killings

One thing is certain, Toronto is experiencing an alarming number of violent deaths of young black men, a fact that is not lost on the embattled black community.

At the funeral of O'Brien Christopher-Reid, a black man gunned down by police in an altercation, some called for an end to the tragic cycle of violence resulting in a rising tide of black shooting victims. 21.

What does race have to do with homicide? Nothing and something it would seem.

Some feel race is irrelevant and should be ignored entirely, even to the point of not mentioning the race/ethnicity of wanted criminals. This of course is absurd. If race/ethnicity is never mentioned, the public will likely assume the wanted suspect is of the majority white population, an unhelpful assumption if the suspect is black.

And some are of the opposite extreme. They believe that race explains many homicides; that black people by nature are more likely to kill. This too is absurd. So-called racial differences are literally only skin deep. We're all the same beneath our epidermis. There is in truth only one race – the human race. Nor is there anything in the genetic make-up or brain circuitry of black people that predisposes them to violent crime. Most, in fact, are law-abiding, productive citizens.

What then do we make of the building body count from murders in Toronto – a disproportionately high percentage committed by members of the minority black population?

Last year, 31 murders – nearly half the year's 65 homicides – were gun-related. That's an increase of more than 50 per cent from the 1990s annual average of 20 shooting deaths. Clearly easy-access to guns is an issue.

Minority Commits Majority of Murders

Nearly all of the 31 gun-related homicides were believed to be gang-related and more than 70 per cent of them involved black gunmen and black victims.

Toronto police would be wrong to ignore such statistics. They wouldn't be doing their job if they turned a blind eye to the fact that a small minority group in the GTA population is involved in more than 70 per cent of gun-related homicides, a trend that has continued during the first half of this year.

Police are wise to keep a watchful eye on groups of black youth that may include known gang members in neighbourhoods where there is a history of gunplay and crime.

But as The Toronto Star's investigative series showed, racial profiling takes an unacceptable turn when it's used as an excuse for groundless discrimination; for stopping black drivers solely on the colour of their skin; for penalizing blacks while letting whites off with a warning.

Such conduct only undermines the black community's trust in the predominantly white police force.

Instead of over-reacting to the statistical evidence – either by rejecting it or by using it as an excuse to harass minority groups – society should employ this evidence towards gaining a deeper understanding of the underlying issues and causes of such violence.

The evidence raises a number of important questions, including the obvious: Why is a small minority group responsible for the majority of gun-related homicides?

Questions Run Deep

But the questions run much deeper: Are Toronto's black offenders drawing inspiration from foreign cultures where murder is more commonplace?

Are they equating Canadian society with American society where shooting deaths are much higher (Chicago is roughly the size of Toronto but had 600 shooting deaths last year – nearly 10 times Toronto's tally)?

Are young blacks encountering real or perceived severe discrimination?

Are some young gunmen products of an impoverished and isolated environment where crime is quietly condoned as retribution against a prosperous society that seems to exclude blacks?

Addressing these questions should reveal the degree of change that needs to take place to stem the rising tide of shootings.

The statistics have served to provide vital information. It's now up to the police and society as a whole to utilize this information constructively to delve deeply into the issues, uncover the root causes and enact whatever measures are necessary to bring about a resolution, and an end to this tragic carnage.

One thing that needs to change is a ridiculous politically correct approach that amounts to putting one's head in the sand. The black factor is either ignored or used as an excuse to go easy on black criminals because society has supposedly wronged black people.

For example, in a recent court case, three women who smuggled large quantities of cocaine into Canada were only given house arrest: confined to their homes except under certain circumstances, such as trips to the grocery store.

Fortunately sanity was restored when an Ontario Court of Appeal judge overruled the lower court and correctly ruled that the women are not entitled to lenient sentences simply because they are black, single mothers living in poverty and having a tough go of things.

Overturning Reverse Discrimination

The Ontario Court of Appeal ruled that a sentencing court is not the place to "right perceived societal wrongs" or "make up for perceived social injustices by the imposition of sentences that do not reflect the seriousness of the crime."

The court found that the women deserved between 20 and 40 months behind bars - even if it meant their children would temporarily be left without mothers.

While the women, who smuggled cocaine through Pearson airport were struggling with hard economic circumstances, they "had a choice to make and they made that choice knowing full well the harm that the choice could cause to the community," said Mr. Justice David Doherty.

I believe the drug mules case illustrates what I see as an underlying factor that serves to perpetuate the role of black people, a small minority, committing the majority of violent crimes.

The sentencing court made a racist decision in favour of the black defendants. It found that because they were black and living in poverty their sentences should be lighter than they'd receive if they were white: Reverse discrimination at its worst. The message: Society sympathizes with black criminals because some are living hard lives in poverty.

It fosters an attitude of acceptance of crime. It sends the message that it's really okay at a moral level for a black person to commit a crime because, well, they're black and therefore have enough to contend with, what with prejudice and discrimination and all that.

This asinine (but to some, politically correct) attitude may be behind the decision of some frustrated youth to resort to guns and knives. If not for this attitude, these young men might otherwise hesitate if they thought it was truly wrong.

Mixed Messages

Instead they're getting mixed messages that suggest the unacceptable is for them acceptable because society owes them something.

So, a young jobless hothead who hasn't looked all that hard for work turns to crime to get even with The Man. Bullets start flying and more tragic murders result.

And the death toll shows no sign of diminishing: During a mid-June 2004 weekend, a knife-wielding black man was shot dead and a policeman wounded in a normally peaceful, scenic park near Toronto's Edwards Gardens. [22.]

According to a Toronto Star report, witnesses said the man appeared to be emotionally disturbed. Police say they opened fire when the man lunged at them with a knife.

Three police officers shot the man to death, prompting one medical professional to state that police are not properly trained when dealing with the mentally ill and that better training might well have prevent a fatality. [23.]

The one police officer who was injured was hit by a stray police bullet. There have been nearly a dozen fatal shooting incidents involving police slaying people, during the eight-year period 1996-2004. [24.]

In some cases, the suspects are literally crazy and therefore unpredictable. They're often former mental patients that the Ontario government feels should be released onto the streets rather than staying institutionalized. So, today's mental patient becomes tomorrow's street person. Unable to find meaningful employment, most live out lives of quiet desperation. A few act out their frustrations – with tragic consequences.

A few days after the park shooting, in an unrelated violent episode, a 42-year-old Toronto man was arrested and charged with attempted murder after a woman and her daughter were beaten with a hammer. The vicious hammer attack – the scene was drenched in blood – took place around 3 am at the home of the victims while they slept. 25.

As if Toronto doesn't have enough home-grown crazies, the city acts as something of a magnet for transients, future homeless babblers and the criminally insane.

People-hater loves Dogs

Take, for example, the case of the New Brunswick man who traveled to Toronto in June 2004 not to visit the CN Tower or take in a Raptors game but to kill people.

The man, an apparently mentally ill dog-lover who didn't like people (four legs good, two legs bad), thought he'd slaughter a lot of innocent people at random so that he could get a place to live and three-square-meals a day for the rest of his life, courtesy of the prison system.

He thoughtfully left his own dog at home in New Brunswick – no point in subjecting his pooch to the screams of dying people, dogs can be pretty sensitive. 26.

Fortunately a friendly mutt wandered by and the man reached the fantastic conclusion that the existence of a friendly dog meant that the people must also be friendly and therefore did not deserve to die. Torontonians can be forever grateful that one of the city's resident non-stop-barking terriers – or worse, vicious pit bulls – didn't wander by or there could have been bloodied bodies piled everywhere. 27.

Indeed, an extremely vicious pit bull attack occurred as recently as late August of 2004. As the Toronto Star's Curtis Rush reports, a 25-year-old man was sent to hospital with "extensive leg, back and arm wounds," after being attacked by two pit bulls in a scene described as an absolute blood bath. 28.

The attack occurred while the man was walking two of the dogs on behalf of the out-of-town owner (later reports suggested the thoughtful owner is a charming individual with a violent streak; neighbours live in fear of the owner and his dogs, all of whom often roamed freely without a leash). The vicious dogs were working their way up the walker's body, heading for his throat despite the desperate efforts of half-a-dozen people to get the pit bulls off him. Police saved the man's life by killing the dogs in a hail of gunfire. 29.

Pit Bull Ban Needed

In an editorial calling for the banning of pit bull ownership, The Toronto Star noted: "At least two small children in the Toronto region were seriously harmed last year," adding: "A person's right to own a pet of his or her choice does not outweigh a community's right to protect itself against dangerous animals, especially in a city where so many of us share the same parks and streets... pit bulls were involved in 65 fatal attacks between 1979 and 1998 (in the U.S.). Almost half of all dog attacks are by pit bulls, yet they make up less than 1 per cent of the canine population." 30.

As for the crazy east-coaster, in town for a little mayhem and recreational killings of human beings, well, as luck would have it, something as irrelevant and happenstance as a playful pooch was all it took to convince the dog-lover-human-hater to give himself up to police.

He was armed with a loaded gun in his pocket and more than 6,000 rounds of ammunition crammed in his car, crowding for space with other weapons – including automatic weapons and shotguns – doggie kibble and dog blankets. Police weren't that impressed with the dog supplies – but it was the largest lethal arsenal they'd ever seen. 31.

What's the answer to Toronto crime?

Part of the answer lies in treating crime more seriously. The Ontario government recently tightened a loophole in the law that allowed doctor-patient confidentiality practices to forget about informing the police when a physician treated someone with a bullet wound. 32.

Doctors were asked to report gunshot wounds but because this wasn't mandatory, too many physicians succumbed to pressure from criminal shooting victims to keep the shooting confidential. This made the job of tracking down criminals involved in gunplay all the more difficult for police encountering a wall of silence from doctors. 33.

Finding Answers to Crime

Now when a robbery or any crime involving a shooting takes place, police will have an easier time tracking down criminals shoot in the course of committing their offence. It's about time this change happened. Hospitals are required to report any cases of suspected child abuse or infectious diseases or unfit drivers – now they must also report gunshot wounds, allowing police to arrest hospitalized lawbreakers shot while committing a crime. 34.

Also in June 2004, a jury convicted Toronto man Adrian Almarales for his role in a horrific killing spree that left two people dead and a third fighting for his life. The shooter, Joseph Prieto, also of Toronto, shot all three people execution style in the head, then killed himself... 35.

At about the same time the shooting spree trial was taking place, the public was reacting to Toronto Mayor David Miller's sudden firing of Toronto police Chief Julian Fantino was drawing mixed reactions from the public. The Toronto Star's Voices feature, allowing readers to vent their opinions, found some readers questioning the wisdom of firing the police chief at a time when the city is finding it difficult to cope with violent crime. Reader Jamal Robinson of Toronto, reflected the worries of many when he noted: "I live in a community that is suffering from violence, and while I have not always agreed with the chief, I truly believe that he was honestly searching for ways to make communities safer while at the same time respecting people's rights." 36.

While most Canadians were celebrating Canada Day, Ricardo Hopeton Brown, 24, was shot to death while visiting friends on the July 1 national holiday.

Brown, a black man, was employed as a warehouse shipper at Purolator Courier. He was also taking courses at Thistletown Collegiate Institute in Toronto's Rexdale community and had planned to study architecture. Described as an all-round good guy, Brown had come to Canada from Jamaica in February 2003. The gunman shot Brown repeatedly as the father of a 3-month-old girl tried to flee the scene. With 2004 barely half-over, he had the dubious honour of becoming Toronto's 30th homicide victim of the year. 37.

More Blacks Die

In the same day's paper, above Brown's black face, was the black face of another shooting victim: Rhoan Gooden, a popular bouncer who was slain in 2002, leaving behind a wife and two children.

His killer, also a black man, was captured on July 2, 2004, by U.S. marshals and charged with the attempted murder and assault of a U.S. marshal. No word on when the killer will be returned to Canada to face first degree murder charges here. 38.

Barely a week later, two thugs were convicted of murder after they hunted their victim – a young black American – like prey, robbing him and wounding him, then chasing the terrified man down Toronto streets before finishing him off with four shots to the head. 39.

The city of Toronto lives in fear of crime, to the point that some will avoid going out at night or seek out extreme security measures for public spaces. Noting Toronto residents are keeping clear of a neighbourhood park at night, the Toronto Star's Andrew Mills and Leslie Ferenc report:

"Fearing an armed sexual predator is on the loose and may return, residents in the city's northwest are demanding Summerlea Park be locked at night after a woman was abducted at gunpoint, robbed and then brutally assaulted in the bushes… It's the fifth attack in the park in about a year. Toronto police believe the same man is responsible. They're warning residents to stay out of Summerlea at night as they hunt for the sexual predator and robber." 40.

Not that all citizens are afraid of fighting back. In yet another horrific crime of violence against the elderly, a 73-year-old man was stabbed in the neck in August, 2004, and was bleeding profusely when two Toronto men rushed to his side and provided life-saving first-aid treatment. 41.

Elderly Attacked

And let's not lose sight of the fact that this was a 73-year-old, elderly senior citizen who was stabbed in the neck by a cowardly assailant.

In yet another horrific crime, an elderly man was stabbed to death. As the Star's Christian Cotroneo reports: "It was closing time when a stranger stepped inside Kenny Kim's downtown convenience store and stabbed him to death. The 63-year-old didn't have much cash in the till that June 18 evening. But he had a rack full of cigarettes." Cotroneo goes on to report that weeks later a 57-year-old man was repeatedly stabbed in the chest for some cash and cigarettes. "At about $66 per carton, cigarettes are fast becoming currency – untraceable, easy to unload on the streets and, unlike the contents of cash registers, easy to snatch." Police estimate at least 15 stores were robbed for cigarettes in a 2-week period – more than one per day." 42.

Let's think about this for a moment: Stabbing someone to death is an extremely vicious way to kill someone. Stabbings, unlike shootings, involve extremely close, personal contact, a great deal of physical exertion. It also involves a strong desire to take the victim's life by forcefully and repeatedly jabbing a sharp object into their vital organs – and it's difficult to imagine the degree of rage and hatred needed to stab to death a total stranger, a helpless senior citizen begging for his life. Stabbing often covers both the victim and killer in the victim's blood. The killer can hear the victim's last gasps of life rasping in his ear.

Now let's think about this vicious crime being committed against elderly people who have done absolutely nothing to provoke it. Grandparents are being stabbed to death for a few lousy packs of cigarettes.

And callous, random shootings are also claiming innocent victims. Is life becoming as cheap in Toronto as it is in most American cities? Let's hope the senseless stabbings and shootings aren't part of a growing mentality in the criminal element to disregard human life while committing petty crimes.

Arguments Lead to Murder

Far too often, it seems, verbal disputes in Toronto rapidly escalate into homicides.

The Toronto Star's Cal Millar recounts one such case in August 2004: "It began as a dispute between a landlord and tenant, turned into a house fire, and by the time was over, two people were in hospital with stab wounds... the 67-yeaqr-old tenant is in critical condition with self-inflicted stab wounds, while the landlord's wife is in stable condition after surgery..." 43.

Crime in Toronto is seemingly everywhere. Even the chief of police can't get away from it during a social visit to the Canadian National Exhibition fairgrounds. As the Toronto Star's Melissa Godsoe and William Lin report: "Only hours after lamenting the loss of a bygone era's peace and quiet, Toronto Police Chief Julian Fantino found himself involved in a dust-up while making an arrest at the CNE." 44.

Chief Makes the Collar

The report goes on to note that Fantino, in full uniform, was at the EX to give a speech on youth violence when someone approached him with a complaint that a man was taking unwanted photos of children.

Fantino confronted the man and a struggle ensued with the police chief pinning and handcuffing the suspect.

It's rare that the police chief gets personally involved in making an arrest, but such as the state of affairs in Toronto. Ironically, the police chief's speech bemoaned the high rate of crime in Toronto and reflected on historically better times when the streets actually were safe. 45.

Indeed, the week before the chief's Monday dust-up, there were several much more serious crimes, including murders. In one case, a 48-year-old bouncer was stabbed to death after he tried to oust some unwanted trouble-makers from a sports bar (four black men were later charged with murder).

In a related incident, a 27-year-old man was stabbed to death in his apartment following an argument.

The week wasn't yet over when there were reports of a teenager admitting he played a role in the murder of his friend's father. Another report disclosed that a man found dead in a grow house had died of a gunshot wound. 46.

By the third week of August 2004, Toronto proper (the city of 2.5 million people before suburbs are added on) had already experienced 40 homicides in what was shaping up to be a record year for killings.

Indeed, two days later, Tony Brookes, a disgruntled black man who cared nothing about the lives of his fellow citizens, attempted unsuccessfully to kill his ex-wife in a crowd of people.

He fired two shotgun blasts at her during rush hour in one of the busiest parts of the city.

After he missed both times and his gun jammed, he beat his wife senseless and ran as police closed in. At Union Station, Brookes grabbed an innocent passer-by and held the terrified woman hostage at gunpoint until a police sharpshooter put the stupid ass out of his misery.

Further killings followed and during the first week of September, a 21-year-old black man, Shemaul Andre Cunningham was shot to death in a drive-by shooting on Highway 401.

It was the city's 44th homicide of the year (police do not believe it was a random shooting), with no sign the ongoing slaughter would let up anytime soon.

Perceptions Crime is out of Control

Bill Dunphy notes that for some time now there has been the widespread appearance, the strong perception, violent crime in Toronto is out of control: "Historically, murder cases here – like most Canadian communities – enjoyed very high clearance rates, with arrests coming in 80 to 90 per cent of all murders.

But that changed at some point over the past two decades, slowly sliding to the point where these days it seems as if you've got a fifty-fifty chance of getting away with murder." 47.

As Dunphy adds: "If you've a regular consumer of Toronto media, you can be forgiven for thinking that people like those odds, so frequent are the reports of shootings and stabbings. They seem to happen so often the horrible details all run together, painting a picture of a city under siege." 48.

Dunphy goes on to note that Toronto's murder rate per 100,000 people is about average for Canadian cities and he observes that your chances of being slain are sharply reduced if you are not involved in gangs or criminal activity of any kind. 49.

Indeed, statistically, Toronto casts the illusion of a safe city, especially compared to American cities, but even when compared to other Canadian cities.

Toronto's 2003 murder rate of roughly 2 murders per 100,000 people was slightly less than Vancouver's rate, significantly less than the 3 murders per 100,000 people in Saskatoon and well behind Abbotsford, B.C. and Regina where the annual murder rate is more than five per 100,000.

Cold Comfort

But this should come as cold comfort to any thinking person. All of the other cities compared that featured higher annual homicide rates are also much smaller than Toronto, Canada's most populous city with a metropolitan population of about 5 million people (with 2.5 million in the city itself)

Toronto is three times the size of Vancouver and at least 20 times larger than any of the other cities named in this comparison.

This means more than 100 people are slain annually in metropolitan Toronto while barely 6 people are killed in "metro" Saskatoon.

This more meaningful comparison is rendered even scarier when you consider Toronto's high population density: The city loves to pack as many people as it possibly can into every square mile – as though trying to win a contest. To live in downtown Toronto is be surrounded by tens of thousands of people in your immediate neighbourhood. This increases the odds that some of those 100-plus metro-wide killings per year will take place in your neighbourhood, perhaps on your block, maybe in your building. Who's that lurking at your doorway? Is someone creeping up behind you?? (I know, I should have tastefully ended this rant at "your building." I apologize. It'll probably never happen again).

Encouraging Signs

Some are also beginning to question the absurd extent to which reverse discrimination has grown. The phobia about saying anything negative about the black criminal element – the leading source of shooting homicides – may finally be subsiding somewhat. Ontario judges have at last come under criticism for deliberately providing overly lenient sentences to blacks purely on the grounds that they're black and therefore supposedly have enough problems to contend with what with being black and having to deal with prejudiced people and all.

It's precisely this attitude that condones and even encourages impoverished blacks to commit crimes on the basis that it's okay to commit serious crimes because society supposedly owes them an apology and a higher standard of living. Fortunately, in the case of the black women smugglers, sanity prevailed and the Ontario Court of Appeal found the sentencing judges were way out of line. The appeal court found that the female "drug mules" made a choice to smuggle dangerous drugs into the community, regardless of their economic situation, and therefore should be adequately punished for committing very serious crimes. 50.

Such cracking down on reverse discrimination is encouraging – crime is crime regardless of one's gender, skin colour or ethnicity.

Also encouraging are the numbers of youth-oriented education, training and employment programs aimed at problem areas – such as Malvern – across Toronto.

This is a realistic effort to resolve some of the social conditions that in some cases lead to crime. Let's hope Toronto continues to take crime and its causes seriously to turn around its severe, entrenched problems of violent crime.

"I hate Toronto but unfortunately I have to business with companies in Toronto so I don't want my name used. I know from dealing with so many Toronto people that it takes both the husband and wife working just to make ends meet and there's a lot of latch-key kids in Toronto, who are left on their own all day. It isn't right. Life shouldn't be that expensive, it shouldn't be so hard just to get by – but it is in Toronto. It's like Toronto is punishing you for living there."

- **Joe** (real name withheld by request)

8

Shattered Dreams

A major reason why so many people hate Toronto is owed to the city's over-priced real estate. My research efforts encountered this simply fact again and again.

Virtually all Canadians aspire to the Canadian dream of home ownership. But in Toronto, the dream often stays just that – a dream – because prices are far too high for anyone of average means to buy a home.

It's just another shattered dream – and it's fuelling resentment towards Toronto.

It leads to people spending their adult years living in their parents' basement well into their 30s while they struggle to set aside an $80,000 25-per cent down-payment on a $320,000 average detached home that's miles away from the job in a bad neighbourhood. And the house needs work.

Sure, they can put less than 25 per cent down and take on a CMHC-insured mortgage that will increase the size of their overall mortgage and the payments they'll have to make.

But let's face it, a 25 per cent down-payment of $80,000 leaves them with a mortgage of nearly a quarter-million dollars that they can't afford anyway. And if they can't afford a $240,000 mortgage, it's a certainty they won't be able to carry a $304,000 mortgage. So much for the dream of owning your own detached house.

Condo sales are booming in Toronto, not because people really like living in condos, but because they can't possibly afford to buy a detached home anywhere worth living in this over-priced city, notorious for having some of the most expensive real estate in Canada.

Incredibly, The Toronto Star lauded the fact that: "Development fees that are levelled against new homes and condominiums are set to double in Toronto. But this 100 per cent increase is more a bargain than a burden. For too long, municipal taxpayers have been stuck with costs that should properly be borne by developers and the buyers of new homes." [1]

The Star editorial went on to note that new developments require new services such as water lines, sewer connections and roads "and new development also imposes less-obvious costs on the city, such as a need for more ambulance coverage. [2]

Municipalities charge a development fee to help pay for expanding services and Toronto city council is boosting these charges to $9,075 for a new house – up from $4,370" while a one bedroom condo's fee jumped to $4,658 from $1,802. [3]

The editorial notes these raised fees are still much lower than the development fees charge elsewhere in the greater Toronto area where the fee for new homes averages nearly $18,000. The editorial concludes that people living in older homes in Toronto are subsidizing those who live in new homes so now the fee hikes help correct an imbalance. [4]

However, it's also safe to say that when this fee hike is added on to the purchase price of a condo unit or home (as it inevitably will be – don't expect developers to eat this cost), we can expect the dream of home ownership will be pushed beyond the grasp of generations of new Torontonians. And what a modest fleeting dream it was: The chance to own a little apartment unit and build up equity you might one day apply as a down payment on a home you really want, a home that can raise a family in. French Canadians might express it this way: You had a dream: There it is. Gone.

Of course the development fee hikes are in addition to maintenance fee increases, which are rising sharply as buyers absorb rising heating and utility costs and increases in water charges and property management fees.

One couple in North Toronto was notified in September 2004 that their monthly condo maintenance fee was going to nearly double to almost $600 per month. I know that sounds like a mortgage payment, but that's just the monthly condo fee. And this couple was being hit with this financial burden only a year after moving into their condo.

In fact, up to 90 per cent of new condo owners are being hit with fee hikes beyond the rate of inflation. Add on the mortgage payments and it can cost thousands of dollars – just to own an apartment!

All of this means life in the big city is getting even more expensive. When condo apartments came into vogue (about the same time tiny detached, rundown shacks soared past the $quarter-million mark), you could pick up a decent-sized one-bedroom condo close to everything for $100,000.

You can now expect to pay double that amount for anything worth living in (some condos are listed at $120,000 – but they're about the size of a walk-in closet or they overlook a polluted highway).

And if little condo apartments are this costly, how expensive is the Canadian dream of owning a fully detached house on a lot with a backyard for the kids? The answer: Very expensive, as in $300,000 on average in the Greater Toronto Area to half-a-million-dollars for an average family home close to the centre of Toronto itself.

Simply put, if you won a million dollars and wanted to stop working but still live in Toronto, your $1-million would barely afford you a little bungalow and an investment income flow equivalent to about $50,000 a year, tops. In other words a million dollars might buy you a modest, middle-class lifestyle in Toronto, while almost anywhere else in Canada you'd be living high off the hog, in style.

As Tony Wong, a Business section reporter for the Toronto Star, noted in the spring of 2004, "It will cost you close to half a million dollars for a standard two-storey home in the Beach district, and more than $1-million if you want a similar home in Midtown Toronto..." 5.

Wong notes the Midtown Toronto area, with its epicentre at Yonge Street and St. Claire Avenue, had an average selling price back in April of 2004 of $1.2 million. This didn't necessarily get you a fully detached house as row houses were commanding more than $1-million. Condo apartments were going for around $250,000. 6.

The average working stiff in Toronto is far from being a millionaire. And with more and more homes costing $1-million or more, and condos costing a $quarter-million, the average Joe is forever relegated to paying inflated rents – or commuting vast distances to work in this punitively expensive city.

New home buyers are looking at rising utility, water/sewer and other costs of running a household, plus the certainty of developers passing along to buyers any increases in development fees.

And, we're now seeing rising mortgage rates. The average five-year mortgage rate in August 2004 rose to nearly 6.5 per cent, a level not seen in many months.

The rate hike prompted the Royal Bank of Canada to release an RBC Economics report raising the affordability index.

It now takes 37.2 per cent of pre-tax income to buy the average home in Toronto. That's an average home, not a $1-million home.

So what precisely does a $1-million get you in terms of a home in Toronto? The Star's Tony Wong went out searching for homes listed at or near $1-million, and he was clearly underwhelmed by his findings. 7.

Wrote Wong: "Let's say you just won a million dollars in the lottery and want to buy a home in downtown Toronto. The good news is, you have a million dollars. The bad news: You only have a million dollars." 8.

Wong discovered that for the most part, $1-million gets you a townhouse. That's it. A townhouse. Hardly the stuff of heady fantasies. More of a mundane reality. 9.

Re/Max reports that sales of million dollar homes in Toronto were up 38 per cent in the spring of 2004 over the spring of 2003. That's hardly surprising when even a lowly, entry-level townhouse without a garage or even a parking spot can command $1.2 million dollars.

And forget about buying anything for $1-million in the more exclusive parts of town such as Forest Hill.

Wong did manage to find one fully detached; downtown Toronto home priced a hair below an even $1-million. It was a small two-storey home on a small lot that boasted an attached ONE-car garage. Similar homes can be found in downtown Hamilton – for about $130,000. 10.

He also found a narrow, three-storey home on a narrow lot – less than 19-feet-wide and 63-feet-deep – with NO-GA-RAGE listed at $1.2 million – about 10 times what you'd pay for the same house in downtown Hamilton. 11.

On the same say as Wong's informative feature, the Star's business section ran its standard little 'What They Got' housing industry snap shot, featuring a tiny bungalow on a 40-foot-lot in Etobicoke. The asking price: $288,000. The selling price: $296,500 – no doubt the outcome of a bidding war, a frequent occurrence in the Toronto market, which serves to drive up prices and dissuade would-be buyers from offering anything less than the full asking price (and pray that that's enough to 'win' the deal).

Toronto's inflated housing prices clearly stunned Bill Dunphy, The Hamilton Spectator's foreign correspondent in Toronto.

Dunphy couldn't believe the little house across the street could command a hefty million-dollar price tag, adding: "Oops, there I go mixing up Toronto with the rest of the world. When we found out we had a million-dollar home on our little street, we realized that Toronto homebuyers had taken leave of their pampered senses. It doesn't even have a garage. Heck it barely even has a back yard." 12.

Dunphy concludes "a million-dollar home conjures up a circular drive, with a manicured land and perhaps a topiary; an indoor swimming pool or bowling alley, outdoor tennis courts and maybe a stone terrace to glide across in the moonlight. A modest mansion. Not in Toronto." 13.

Even if a homeowner decides to list their home at a more reasonable price, it's likely a bidding war will erupt that will serve to drive the selling price ever higher. For example, an ordinary-looking home in Toronto's west end was recently listed at $649,000 as the asking price (the same house would fetch about $250,000 in Hamilton's west end). This $649,000 home sold for $728,000 – or about $80,000 MORE than the vendor was willing to accept in his wildest dreams. 14.

Offering the full asking price often isn't enough any more. Chances are someone will come along and outbid you. This of course further skews the affordability situation as prices are pushed ever further out of reach of ordinary people. 15.

And waiting lists for affordable-housing units in Toronto snow stretch for 15 years. Who can wait that long? Faced with a lack of affordable housing, no down payment for a home and expensive rents, a once-bearable temporary job loss is now enough to push more and more Torontonians onto the streets to join the ranks of the homeless.

But there's no let up to rising resale house prices in sight, not as long as some can pay the toll.

Not surprisingly, new home prices are also going through the roof. A new subdivision in the Stouffville area of Greater Toronto has prices starting at $900,000 and rising to more than $1-million. But the crowning touch in this new development is the 32,000-square-foot, Castle of Lords, complete with bowling alley, squash court, ballroom, eight bedrooms, two kitchens, two dining rooms, a library, a conservatory, video arcades, billiards room, home theatre and asking price of $11-million. 16.

Of course, that pales compared to the $13-million a Toronto resale home fetched in 2003. It was the highest priced home in all the Toronto that year. But the following year, its $13-million value placed it a poor third on Toronto's list of expensive homes.

As the Toronto Star's Tony Wong notes, $1-million doesn't get you a lot of house. And million-dollar price tags are becoming far more common. Nearly 470 homes costing a million dollars or more changed hands in the first five months of 2004, an increase of nearly 50 per cent over the same timeframe in 2003.

Wong also observes that the average price of a home in Toronto, including all types of housing, even fixer-uppers, stood at $325,000 in the spring of 2004. 17.

As if to prove his point, the same day that Wong's report appeared, The Star also ran a real estate item reporting that a home with an asking price of $319,900 actually sold for $330,000 – another outcome of bidding wars that can spring up without notice in the hot real estate market. 18.

By the way, first place for most expensive home in Toronto in 2004 went to a $25-million mansion in the city's exclusive Rosedale neighbourhood. The home is the most expensive in Toronto history and features eight bedrooms, 13 washrooms and an indoor six-car garage. 19.

If that's a little rich for your blood, another estate project, in north Toronto offered homes for around $1.3-million each. 20.

And there's no evidence the real estate market in Toronto is about to cool off. In the spring of 2004, prices had climbed more than 9 per cent for standard two-storey homes, compared with spring of 2003. The average price for this type of housing is now approaching half-a-million dollars. 21.

By mid-September, 2004, Wong was reporting a 43 per cent increase in million-dollar deals. Describing a pair of very costly homes, Wong reports:

> "The contemporary manor in one of Toronto's most elegant neighbourhoods had everything a home-owner could want, including seven bedrooms and bathrooms and parking for six cars. It had a price tag to match, costing the buyer $6.7 million. The Forest Hill home... was only one of 751 homes valued at more than a million dollars that sold in the Toronto area during the first eight months of the year, up 43 per cent from the same time last year... One of the most expensive listings in Toronto is a new stone mansion on 0.81 hectare in the Bridle Path area. It lists for $12.9 million..." 21.

One source of less expensive but highly desirable housing is Toronto Island. However, it's next to impossible to buy a home there. The waiting lists are 500 would-be islanders long – and even getting on the list is akin to winning the lottery. Of course being on the list only means that should the 499 people ahead of you all manage to buy homes on the island, you would then get your chance. The reality is that very few homes ever come up for sale. For most people, an escape to a lush green island off the shore of Toronto (and with a magnificent view of the city) remains nothing more than a pipe dream.

As a staff journalist with The Toronto Star, I've reported on one option that does bring home ownership within reach of many Torontonians: condominium apartments.

I've reported that the 25 per cent down payment on a half-million-dollar home can buy a condo apartment outright.

Even if you make a more modest down payment, the mortgage carrying costs are often comparable to rent and a condo in the inner city can spare you from commuting or even needing a car at all. You may be able to save substantial by walking to work or taking public transit. Many condo apartments are also near shopping, parks and other amenities.

However, for most Canadians a condo apartment is a poor man's version of the Canadian dream of home ownership. Yes you do own the apartment unit, but where's the backyard for the kids to play in? Where's the safe neighbourhood free of junkies and hookers filling that nearby park? Where's the quiet slice of suburbia with safe schools, friendly neighbours, backyard barbeques and little traffic? For too many Torontonians, the dream of family home remains just that, a dream – unless they move to suburbia and take on the soul-crushing, daily grind of commuting to work.

Even in suburbia, there's little chance of escape. Tony Wong observes that suburban Oakville, a good 20-30 minutes west of downtown Toronto, is awash in pricey real estate.

Wong notes a $15-million Oakville mansion is "the most expensive home ever listed on the Toronto Real Estate Board's Multiple Listing Service for the area." 22.

Of course this $15-million, 20,000-square-foot, waterfront mansion with indoor pool, home theatre and elevator, pales in comparison to the privately-listed waterfront palace of Microsoft Canada president Frank Clegg. 23.

With 26,000 square feet of space, stone wine cellar, 12 fireplaces, multi-level theatre and breath-taking view of Lake Ontario, it pretty much has everything, including a 10,000-square-foot coach house (about 5-6 times the square footage of an executive home). The estate was once owned by William Eaton, of

Eaton department stores fame. His dinner guests included then prime minister William Lyon Mackenzie King. It's believed to carry a $29-million price tag, "a record asking price for a property in Canada," reports Wong. 24.

Also not included in the board's MLS listings are mansions currently being built such as recently fired Nortel chief executive Frank Dunn's mansion reportedly worth $15-million.

Not to be outdone, another former big corporate executive is building a monster home on a four-acre lakeside site. The huge, 48,000-square-foot (scaled back from 54,000-square-feet after neighbours complained) home of Hugo Powell, retired head of Interbrew, owners of Labatts, has to be seen to be believed. And Powell's shopping mall-sized home is estimated to cost more than $16-million. 25.

Wong reports that many of these homes are so huge they resemble European castles – and are attracting crowds of tourists. And you know the world – or at least the Toronto suburb of Oakville – has gone crazy when real estate agents start referring to 10,000-square-foot mansions as cabins.

In August 2004, Oakville had nearly 90 properties list for sale with price tags of $1-million or more. And these are primarily resale properties, not new homes or privately built homes. 26.

The multi-millionaire owners of these million-dollar-plus mansions are helping to drive up overall property values and property taxes in Oakville. In fact, property values have risen nearly 30 per cent in the course of a single year. That's good news for millionaires. Unfortunately, not everyone living in Oakville is quite that wealthy.

Wong cites former Oakville mayor Harry Barrett's complaint that his little bungalow is valued at $650,000. That might be comforting to Barrett – if he didn't have to pay $7,200 a year in property taxes just to live in a little bungalow. His sky-high taxes are thanks to nearby mansions that have driven up real estates values – and taxes – throughout the area. 27.

Other suburban centres are also experiencing heady increases in housing prices, placing home ownership well beyond the reach of many young families. You have to live a long way outside of Toronto to get a family home at an affordable price. Of course you're then looking at the horrendous costs of commuting to Toronto.

A familiar dream for many Canadians for generations has been to buy their own home and later also purchase a cottage, a few hours north of Toronto. After many years of using the cottage as a summer retreat from the city, the owners would retire and move to the cottage to live there year-round as their principal residence. Their former home would then be sold, with the proceeds invested and returns utilized for retirement income. That was the dream and the reality for many. Now that dream has become shattered for this generation and likely all those generations to follow.

As Joseph Brean reported in The National Post, average cottage prices are now in excess of $200,000 and often cost much more in Ontario's Muskoka cottage district after major price increases. Now, owning a modest cottage is beyond the reach of those of average means. As Brean concludes: "Cottaging is an increasingly elite pastime." 28.

And the great escape to the cottage to "get away from it all," is fast becoming just another broken dream for all but the very wealthy. The Toronto Star's Tracy Hanes interviewed Nik Luka, an environmental planner who obtained the viewpoints of nearly 500 cottagers while researching the effects of development on cottage country.

Luka found that with many seasonal cottages being converted to permanent homes and a boom in new residential waterfront construction... exuburbia (the edge of the metropolitan area) is quickly incorporating most of cottage country... It's not unusual for taxes on waterfront properties to exceed $10,000 a year in Muskoka and some owners of larger properties there may pay as much as

$20,000... There is a feeling that the common man is being squeezed out and cottage country is becoming a playground for the wealthy." 29.

The Globe and Mail was finding much the same phenomena at work. Describing cottager Bob Topp's escalation in property taxes, The Globe's Anthony Reinhart reports: "Taxes were $12.95 in 1950, as shown on an old yellowed bill he keeps in a frame. Last year, they were $6,000 thanks to a sudden surge in demand for waterfront property that began in the early 1990s and has quickened since. 30.

In conclusion, most detached houses are beyond the reach of the average person, condos are also becoming too costly for many. Nor are the Toronto islands or suburbia or cottage country viable options due to their rising prices.

This leaves people to house their families in distant communities and make the grinding, soul-destroying commute to Toronto, shackling their lives to long work days.

And the seething resentment over lost dreams continues to fester and grow.

Homeless Problems

The most extreme evidence of Toronto's housing crisis is its growing difficulty in dealing with the homeless.

Simply put, Toronto has no idea how to solve its homelessness problem. Walk down any major street and you nearly trip over the homeless.

Drive down these streets and homeless people swarm up on your vehicle, eager to squeegee clean your windows with water of questionable quality in exchange for a toonie. At night, the homeless curl up on the sidewalks or park benches or they disappear under bridges and makeshift shanty towns.

In May 2004, a number of these drifters suddenly found their shanties demolished. They had been living under a bridge in shacks of cardboard and plywood. Although the city offered to try and help them find someplace else to live, the municipal bureaucrats had nothing in particular in mind.

And their offer came after the shanties were torn down for being in violation of municipal building codes. Shacks in violation of codes?

What a surprise – if the shack dwellers were skilled builders, they wouldn't be living in a shack under a bridge. Toronto Star reporter Andrew Mills observed:

> "For more than two months, the only roof over Luke O'Hearn's head has been... a Bathurst St. bridge. But yesterday morning, O'Hearn watched as a team of 20 city workers used a pair of bulldozers to tear down the crude shelter of old tarps and sheets of plywood. 'I was still asleep when they came this morning to tell me I had five minutes to get out,' he said." 31.

O'Hearn was one of the lucky ones. The bureaucrats managed to find an apartment for him and his girlfriend that they can carry on their monthly welfare cheques. It helps that nearly 4 per cent of Toronto's apartments are vacant.

However, of the dozens of squatters living under the bridge, only 10 agreed to let the city try to find them other accommodations. Perhaps it's difficult to trust authorities that bulldoze your home before holding out a helping hand.

As well, the odds of actually finding a place are remote despite the high vacancy rate: More than 73,000 households in Toronto are currently waiting for subsidized housing and while it's not known how many people are living on the streets, nearly 32,000 people have been making use of city emergency shelters each year. 32.

Not surprisingly, Toronto's sky-high rental and ownership housing costs are also making life difficult for those who have fled oppressive countries in search of a new start in Canada.

As the Toronto Star's Debra Black noted, one fairly typical family of refugees admitted to being stressed out about trying to cover $800 monthly rent for a rundown apartment on $1,000 in monthly support. That left the Afghani family very little disposable income for groceries and other living costs. 33.

So severe are the costs of living in Toronto – especially for new immigrants – just getting settled – that there are reports of newcomers sending their children back to the country they came from to live with relatives, because they can't afford to support their kids right here in Toronto.

I know it sounds incredible, but it's true, and it's a sad state of affairs when children are sent back to China or India or other nations because Toronto, the Promised Land, offers so little that's affordable for those on modest incomes.

The high cost of living is just one of the problems facing newcomers to Canada and Toronto. Some unscrupulous Toronto men use the threat of deportation to trap women into staying in abusive, violent and degrading relationships. The dreams of a wonderful life in Canada are shattered when these women are faced with their Toronto husbands' blackmail threats of calling in immigration authorities to bring about deportation. 34.

There are whole communities in Toronto that primarily consist of people, who, for one reason or another have not been accepted as immigrants, have never qualified, or have lost this status, as in the case of some of the abused immigrant women.

These hidden residents are without records of residency. They hide from the authorities and live in fear of getting caught and deported. Their children either cannot go to school or attend using false identification. The parents may work but are sometimes exploited by employers who know they can pay less than minimum wage, avoid paying overtime and dismiss the worker without cause, because the workers have no legal recourse.

These hidden, unofficial immigrants number in the hundreds, if not thousands. Most contribute to society but cannot access societal benefits such as health care and financial/legal assistance programs. They eke out an existence, living on the margins of society.

An immigration amnesty of some kind is needed to accommodate these primarily hard-working people and welcome them in from the fringes of society.

But few live further out on the fringes of society than Toronto's rapidly growing homeless population. The sad fact remains that many of the homeless are young Canadians who came to Toronto in search of jobs, only to find no employment prospects and an expensive city that is far to costly for them to take up residence. And so they take to the streets and make a rough, makeshift home in ravines, deep in parks, in the covered walkway by Union Station and under roadway bridges.

The homelessness problem has been going on for so long that many in this unofficial community no longer regard this hard lifestyle as something temporary in nature. Instead, they've put down roots of sorts, fashioning makeshift homes out of cardboard boxes, wooden crates and discarded furniture.

At one such community under the Spadina bridge, a security gate has been erected by the residents.

Inside, they relax on discarded couches and chairs, while a cardboard box serves as a coffee table. An Astroturf carpet adds a finishing touch to this rough-hewn 'Shantytown' where conversations are often drowned out by the roar of overhead traffic. 35.

The Toronto Star's Catherine Porter reported that the City's normal response is to attempt to place such homeless people in some of the city's available, official shelters. But Shantytown residents find more safety and security in these makeshift outdoor communities than they could ever hope to find at city shelters. 36.

As Porter recounts:

"At Shantytown, a row of a dozen tents and makeshift lean-tos huddle beneath the... bridge. About

20 young people live here, when they are not panhandling or squeegee-ing car windshields at intersections. They sleep on old mattresses and venture... into the bush beside the railway tracks to relieve themselves... The biggest threat isn't the regular visits by police... It's the threat of eviction by the city." 37.

Clearly Toronto's official shelters for the homeless aren't viewed as an option for the squatters who cite fears of being beaten, raped and robbed by the violent criminals who frequent such shelters.

In contrast, Shantytown gives them a sense of security. As Porter adds:

"It might not look like much, but people feel safe here (according to Dale, the group's leader). They've padlocked the door, so only residents with keys can get in. They've decided on rules – outlawing crack and injection drugs. When one resident started harassing the young women, the group decided to evict him. All of this is better than shelters where fights and theft are common, Dale says. Another resident, who left Winnipeg for Toronto and hopes of a better life, is quoted as stating she doesn't want to risk getting raped and robbed and feels safer sleeping under a bridge with people she knows." 38.

To its credit, Toronto is grappling with housing options to alleviate the struggle of the homeless.
As Toronto Star columnist Carol Goar observes, the Deep Quong Manor is a humane response to the standard, ineffective approach of warehousing hard-to-house people:

"For 15 years, local activists have been operating the refurbished boarding house on Beverley Street. Its tenants include former street people, individuals with mental illness, aboriginal youth, the vulnerable elderly and others fighting back from adversity. What is remarkable about Deep Quong Manor – named after a respected Vietnamese elder – is how inviting it is. The 149-year-old residence is beautifully decorated and impeccably maintained. Most passers-by don't even realize that it is transitional housing." 39.

Goar notes efforts are underway to replicate this success by converting a building on Murray Street into an 86-unit housing project providing accommodations suitable for all hard-to-house people, including those with disabilities, making it an example of "everything that is positive and humane about urban living."
    She points out:
        "None of this would be possible without the open-mindedness of two government agencies. The first is Toronto Community Housing Corporation, landlord for the city's 57,500 social housing units. It has agreed to lease the Murray Street building and rent it back to the Deep Quong citizens' group. The second is Social Development Canada, underwriting the renovations." 40.

As encouraging as these examples of flexible and innovative housing solutions are, much more is needed on a far broader scale to fully address this problem.
    Still, these housing solutions provide insightful prototypes of what should be possible throughout Toronto.
    Thomas Axworthy, the one-time federal government heavy-weight and advisor to former Prime Minister Pierre Trudeau, feels the homeless problem in Toronto and elsewhere is serious enough to warrant national remedies.
    Axworthy, now chairman of the Centre for The Study of Democracy at Queen's University, notes a great deal of progress was made during the Trudeau years when Canada Mortgage and Housing Corporation struck deals with the provinces in the 1970s

and added around 12,000 social units annually to the housing stock. As Axworthy notes: "Paul Martin (former finance minister now Prime Minister) said it best in his 1990 Liberal task force report Finding Room: 'All Canadians have the right to decent housing in decent surroundings at affordable prices.'" 41.

Noting that non-profit housing, co-op housing and grants for starter homes were all part of the successful social mix, Axworthy is calling on Martin to again move ahead with addressing basic housing needs and restore a goal that has been badly derailed.

Axworthy adds: "This affirmation of the centrality of shelter was thrown away in the neo-conservative mania that swept Canada in the mid-1980s. Its nadir was reached in 1995 when (former Ontario premier) Mike Harris cut social assistance by 22 per cent, then froze rates at this low level as taxes were cut for everyone else." 42.

Axworthy notes: "In Toronto, 73,000 people are on a waiting list for subsidized housing and more than 100,000 Torontonians pay more than 50 per cent of their income for shelter." 43.

He observes efforts are now underway to "provide decent shelter to 600,000 to 700,000 Canadians in need," over a decade, but that such efforts are slow getting off the ground and are badly under-funded.

Axworthy asserts: "We should help first those who need help most: This requires that we end the blight of homelessness. Just about the time the federal government withdrew from poverty reduction, Canadians began to notice desperate men and women sleeping on grates. Toronto had one emergency shelter in the 1980s, now the city spends $125-million to provide transitional shelter to the poorest of the poor… the homeless need a team approach to services but most of all they need a home… we need permanent housing for the 7,000 in shelters." 44.

Now let's revisit the unfolding debate over a "new Deal"

for urban Canada, in which the notion of special status for Toronto has emerged.

With its bloodless focus on tax dollars and political powers, the human element in this debate is oddly absent.

It would seem to make sense that to adequately address the issue of homelessness in Toronto and elsewhere, senior levels of government should invest more power and funding at the municipal level, which is closest to the problem.

For example, in Toronto, the Social Housing Services Corporation along with local shelters and social services agencies, together form the front lines contending with this issue.

Since Toronto pays billions of dollars to upper levels of government in taxes, it should logically have a say for this pay, especially when it comes to key, predominantly local issues such as social housing. Unfortunately this aspect so far appears to be left out from the "New Deal" debate.

Goar has also been watching this debate unfold and finds some voices that deserve to be heard are instead missing:

> "A great city needs an arresting skyline, but it also needs wheelchair-friendly sidewalks. It needs a solid tax base, but it also needs a strong sense of community. It needs an economy that is firing on all cylinders, but it also needs sturdy safety nets." 45.

Until the ongoing debate begins to address these issues, the people side of the equation will be left unanswered and the goal of creating a truly liveable city will remain forever on hold.

For now, the inequity continues: The Canadian Housing Observer 2004 report released by Canada Mortgage and Housing Corp. found almost 16 per cent of households live in unacceptable housing that's over-crowded, in disrepair or too expensive for the householder's means.

The average price for a new low-rise house in Toronto was $348,022 at the start of September 2004, almost 8 per cent higher than the $322,645 average for 2003. And Toronto's average condominium price rose 1 per cent to $211,707 from $210,603 in 2003.

Poverty

Poverty exists throughout Toronto, including some of the wealthiest neighbourhoods.

Toronto civic wards with the highest percentage of households earning less than $20,000 a year include Ward 28: Toronto Centre-Rosedale.

Despite having "Rosedale" in its name, much of this ward is far from wealthy. It encompasses Regent Park, Moss Park, Corktown and Toronto Island.

Similarly, Ward 14: Parkdale-High Park is poverty stricken despite the inclusion of lofty "High Park" in its name.

This ward takes in the landscape between Keele Street./ Parkside Drive. and the CN tracks, south to the lakeshore.

It's no surprise that the list includes Ward 8: York West, which runs centres on Finch Ave. W. and runs from Highway 400 through Jane St. and on to Dufferin St.

All told, the list takes up 7 wards and a substantial portion of Toronto real estate.

As the Toronto Star's Kerry Gillespie reports, there are many affluent-appearing areas of Toronto that hold pockets of poverty and the situation may be getting out of control:

> "Unless governments act now, a report warns, many suburban Toronto neighbourhoods are at risk of becoming a lot like American-style ghettos... In 1981 there were just 15 high-poverty neighbourhoods in the former municipalities of Etobicoke, North York, Scarborough, York and East York. By 2001, that number had risen to 92... The minimum wage had, until recently, been frozen since 1995. Disability and unemployment

benefits became more difficult to obtain and welfare rates were slashed. Yet rents in Toronto have skyrocketed more than 30 per cent since 1997. Incomes that are too low, housing costs that are too high and not enough funding for immigrant services and social programs are behind all the poverty statistics, said NDP MP Marilyn Churley. "This is such a devastating. Bleak picture of poverty in one of the richest cities in the world," she said." 46.

Single parents on social assistance in Toronto are finding it increasingly difficult to get jobs, according to a survey carried out for the city's social services division.

The findings are contained in the Social Assistance and Social Exclusion report, which paints a dismal picture for single-parent families. It concludes they have run out of food, are struggling to pay the rent, cannot access the child care that will allow them to look for work or keep their jobs, and are left feeling isolated and without support. 47.

The report also says single parents have not been well served by Ontario Works, a social-assistance program introduced in 1997 by the former Conservative government. The program aims to move social-assistance recipients into the labour market as quickly as possible and imposes sanctions on those who do not participate in mandatory work-related activities. "Past research has shown that work-first social-assistance programs are best suited for reconnecting well-educated, experienced clients with the labour market during periods of low unemployment," the report says. "A program that encourages single parents to move rapidly into the labour market without adequately helping them to address the multiple obstacles they are confronting will have little on-going success."

A major theme of the report - based on a survey of 800 people last year - is that more single parents are facing obstacles to joining the workforce compared with those surveyed five years earlier. 48.

Those roadblocks include a lack of education and skills, lack of child care, a need to care for other family members, physical and mental-health issues, and a lack of Canadian certification and experience. Single parents are also disadvantaged, according to the report, because a "changing labour market" demands a level of education, skills and experience that many of them just don't have to land a job.

In 1995, there were about 25,000 people in Toronto's homeless shelters. By 2002, the number had jumped to 32,000. Homelessness has hit record-setting levels throughout Ontario over the same time.

By sheer coincidence, the Mike Harris government canceled affordable housing programs starting in 1995 (a cumulative loss of more than 90,000 homes as of 2004). The Harris legacy also includes cuts in housing allowances to welfare recipients and a gutting of tenant protection laws. Such measures resulted in numerous poverty-stricken households being evicted from their apartments, some to begin new lives living in cardboard boxes on city streets.

There are signs Toronto is moving to address its housing crisis, at least to some degree. In August of 2004, Toronto City Council approved the establishment of affordable housing projects in half-a-dozen different neighbourhoods.

Although it's a modest beginning, the projects were seen as an important step in accommodating ex-psychiatric patients and others who would be homeless if not for subsidized housing units.

As the Toronto Star's Paul Moloney notes: "Council recently voted to invest $13.6 million in six housing projects across the city, totalling 312 new homes. No one is saying that number will solve the crisis, what with 32,000 people using the city's emergency shelters at some point each year, but it does reflect a new determination to confront not-on-my-backyard attitudes when necessary." 49.

But a lot more needs to be done. Poverty in Toronto neighbourhoods has dramatically intensified, particularly in the inner suburbs, according to a report released in April by the United Way of Greater Toronto.

The United Way report also notes: The number of 'poor' families in Toronto increased by almost 69 per cent between 1981 and 2001.

And there has been a dramatic increase in the number of higher poverty neighbourhoods in Toronto. In 1981, there were 30 such neighbourhoods; 20 years later, there were 120.

This increase has been especially acute in the inner suburbs - the former municipalities of Scarborough, North York, Etobicoke, York and East York - where the combined total of higher poverty neighbourhoods rose from 15 in 1981 to 92 in 2001.

The population of poor immigrant families living in higher poverty neighbourhoods has grown from 19,700 in 1981 to 115,100 in 2001. Immigrant families accounted for two-thirds of the total family population living in higher poverty neighbourhoods.

The child poverty rate has also increased, from one in four in 1990 to one child in three in 1995. [50.]

One in three Toronto children is living in poverty, compared with one in four nationally, and a coalition seeking to eradicate the problem says the situation has worsened.

Child poverty in Toronto now stands at 33.5 per cent, says Toronto Campaign 2000, a group of advocates seeking implementation of the federal resolution to get rid of child poverty by 2000. The group studies the problem of child poverty in Ontario and releases a report card each year.

The median yearly income of poor single-parent families fell to $13,000 in Toronto, while the median income of poor two-parent families fell to $14,040.

Nearly one in three families in Toronto is a lone-parent family, compared with one in four for Ontario and Canada, the group says. The advocacy group also found that while the number of people in Toronto on social assistance dropped since 1995, only half are better off financially. Many get part-time jobs in unstable areas of the labour market and are more vulnerable to layoffs, the group said. They said 20 per cent who get off welfare are back on it within a year.   51.

As well, many of Toronto's poor turn to food banks and soup kitchens in order to survive. But this too has proven to be an imperfect stopgap to a deeply entrenched problem.

As The Toronto Star's Paul Choi reports:

> "The Daily Bread Food Bank, an agency that feeds more than 100,000 hungry patrons a month in the GTA, is facing a critical shortage of food. And that may mean thousands of children will be returning to school with empty stomachs. The food bank reports that its summer virtual food drive, an online-based donating service, has been woefully behind in contributions. Donations are less than one-third of what they were at the same point last summer, says Sue Cox, Daily Bread's executive director. "At this current pace, we'll have a very hard time filling the empty spaces on the Daily Bread's shelves with food," Cox said. "A lot of adults who depend on this service will go hungry. And a lot of children will be returning to school hungry."   52.

Yet the demand for food banks is steadily increasing to the point where as many as 50,000 families in the Greater Toronto Area use food banks.

And many find they have no other choice due to the overwhelming cost of rent. The Star's William Lin reports:

> "Food bank users who live in market-priced housing spend, on average, 75 per cent of their incomes on rent, according to a report released by the Daily Bread Food Bank, a charity that distributes food to individuals through 190 food programs in the GTA. Thirty per cent is considered a healthy percentage, while 50 per cent raises

the "risk of homelessness," says the agency... The increase in the rent of food bank users is much higher than inflation. From 1998-2003, food bank users living in market-priced housing saw their rents rise 16.7 per cent, compared to 12.6 per cent inflation, the report says... Food bank clients in market-priced housing earn 22 per cent more than those in subsidized housing, but pay 198 per cent more in rent... The average income of food bank users in the GTA is $11,160.... Only 3 per cent of food bank users own their own property. Half of food bank clients, and one-third of their children, go hungry at least once a week... more than 20,000 children are living in "cramped and unhealthy" places... The report recommends that governments continue investing in affordable housing and reform such income-security programs as tax credits and employment insurance. 53.

Nor can you write food bank users as lazy individuals or chronic welfare recipients eager to receive public handouts. Food bank statistics show that of the people who use Toronto's food banks, 37 per cent of the new Canadians have a post-secondary education, and 38 per cent of users come from households where at least one person is working. It really breaks the stereotype of who uses a food bank, notes Sue Cox, Daily Bread's executive director, commenting on the results of an annual survey of 1,200 clients in the GTA. "Too many people still think those using the food banks are lazy. What we've really got is some really ambitious people, eager to get ahead, that need extra help." 54.

Unaffordable Tuition Rates

As if the shattered dreams of home ownership and achieving a decent lifestyle weren't enough, Toronto is also afflicted with yet another shattered dream: The high cost of post-secondary tuition rates and related high costs of education leave many putting dreams of a broader formal education on hold – forever.

This isn't just a Toronto problem. But as with so many societal problems, it's infinitely worse in Toronto than in other parts of the country.

Students in Hamilton may also struggle with the high cost of tuition, but they're far more likely to cope given that they have superior access to affordable rents and a lower cost of living.

But in Toronto, the high cost of everything, combined with expensive tuition is enough to make post-secondary education a non-starter for far too many would-be students.

Commenting on outrageous increases in tuition rates, a Toronto Star editorial dulyn noted that: "No matter what their major, every Ontario university and college student returning to class this month should take a crash course in advanced finance. That's because their tuition fees have tripled over the last 15 years. At the same time, government loan maximums have been frozen for a decade, leaving more students struggling to make up the difference through their own or their parents' savings or by going deeply into debt." 55.

"What has happened to Ontario's dream of affordable post-secondary education for anyone who is qualified?" The Star questions, then asks:

"And what can the government and institutions do to restore that goal? Over the last decade, a fundamental proposition of our post-secondary education system - that taxpayers pay - has been turned on its head. Our cash-strapped government, which has traditionally shouldered much of the bill, is shifting more of the cost to students, without increasing financial aid to those who need it... if the broader trend toward fee increases resumes, our long-cherished principle of accessibility will be undermined, leaving universities and colleges an option only for the wealthy... the current system in Ontario is forcing students to pay more of the overall cost of their education than ever." 56.

As the Star editorial also noted:

"College students now pay about $1,800 per year and university students will pay an average of $4,960 this year. In deregulated programs such as medicine and law, fees are even higher. Those rates are more than double what they were in the early 1990s. On top of tuition, living expenses and other fees can push annual costs easily to $18,000-$20,000 a year for some students. Despite rising tuition and other expenses, the maximum amount of federal and provincial loans available to a single student has been capped at $9,350 per year since 1994. For many, that means turning to bank loans and credit lines because employment income, family contributions and institutional grants and scholarships aren't enough. Students who need to get loans are graduating now with an average debt of $20,000..." 57.

And it's not just tuition that has hit unaffordable levels. Textbooks are also weighing in with hefty price tags that can make dreams of a university education evaporate.

The Toronto Star's Louise brown reports:

"In a corner of the Ryerson University courtyard... second-year students Jessica Molina and Karen Ho arranged to make a sale to two first-year students they had met the day before. The transaction? Textbooks, the hidden expense of higher education. On top of homesickness and workload and soaring tuition fees, students are grappling this month with the sticker-shock of their book lists. "Every dollar counts when you're spending up to $1,000 a year on nursing textbooks," said Molina, a returning student who approached several first-year students in a bookstore last week along with classmate Karen Ho to offer their old first-year texts at a discount. They had a deal. With the average university student in Canada spending about $800 a year on textbooks… students are scrambling to save money, especially on big-ticket tomes in science, business and engineering that can cost more than $150 apiece… Political science major Katherine Bowers dropped $463 for the 14 books in her cart… Commerce freshman Frances Yi paid $332 for four books… after spending almost $200 the day before… Science student Antonella Racano paid $342.83 for the books for just two courses, biology and biochemistry, with a $120 physiology text yet to buy. She already has spent $80 on novels for a course on major British writers. "I've spent about $420 for this term on books - which is about the same as the actual cost of a half-course," she said…" 58.

Jesse Greener, Ontario chairperson of the Canadian Federation of Students, says there is a common refrain echoing through the halls of Ontario's colleges and universities: "We urgently need significant reinvestment in post-secondary education." 59.

"As it stands," Greener notes, "per capita spending in Ontario ranks last in Canada. Federal and provincial funding has dramatically declined over the past decade, ushering in a succession of acute tuition fee hikes. As Statistics Canada notes, tuition fees have nearly tripled since 1990. And while Queen's Park should be commended for fully funding a tuition fee freeze for the next two years, Ontario students still pay the second highest fees in Canada - an average of $4,960… Some… have suggested that rising tuition fees do not diminish access to post-secondary education so long as students can borrow freely and pay back their loans at a later date. But this model ensures that those who come to the table with the least are forced into the deepest debt." 60.

According to Greener, proponents of this regressive model close their eyes to the real impact of rising tuition fees and debt on students from low and modest means. He notes:

"The truth is, between 1993 and 1994 and 1998-'99 - the period when tuition fees increased the fastest in Ontario - post-secondary enrolment rates actually declined. In 2001, there were 825,400 full and part-time students enrolled in post-secondary education in Canada, a figure still below the record set in 1992-'93... Human Resources Development Canada suggests that fully three-quarters of all new jobs created will require some post-secondary education. This makes college and university education a matter of economic survival, not a frivolous add-on for a minority of people, or a one-way ticket to affluence. Most people hope their children will pursue post-secondary education. Yet the reality is only about 60 per cent of young people between the ages of 25 and 34 do so..." 61.

One thing is clear: Something will have to be done about sky-rocketing tuition rates and book costs, along with other high costs of living in Toronto, or new generations will simply fall by the wayside. And they'll all hate Toronto.

"They've got a great location; right on the lake, but they block the view with a bunch of condos. It's ridiculous."

Gene Mason,
Survey participant, Hamilton, Ontario.

"I don't like diesel with my dog. What do I mean by that? I'm saying I don't like to taste diesel or gasoline fumes when I order a hot dog from one of those street venders. It's bad enough having to breathe in Toronto, having to suck in their air pollution every time you breathe, without having to taste it in your food. I live near industry in Hamilton so I'm used to some pollution but the extreme air pollution in Toronto is disgusting.

Jim Sibley, survey participant, Hamilton

"I hate Toronto because it's Toronto, a big cold city full of strangers in a rush to get somewhere else. I also hate the violence there, the street gangs – and the Argos suck."

Wendy Sibley, survey participant, Hamilton.

9

The Unliveable City

Pollution is terrible in Toronto, far worse than in Hamilton, despite the Steel City's smoke-belching factories.

Indeed, pollution index readings routinely rate Toronto's air as being of poorer quality than Hamilton's air.

In the Steel City, much of the pollution is contained in The Hammer's industrial north-east end.

But in Toronto, pollution is everywhere. Toronto's traffic choked streets and highways ensure cars are kept idling for extended periods of time, maximizing the amount of exhaust fumes choking the air, which can actually be difficult to breathe – especially if you have asthma or a breathing disorder of any kind. And Toronto gets an average of at least 14 poor air quality days every year.

In early June 2004, Toronto smog was at literally sickening levels. It stung my eyes and burned my lungs as I commuted to the Toronto Star, into a city shrouded in thick smog.

Oppressive heat and a van air conditioning system that didn't work meant keeping the windows down as I breathed in the exhaust of bumper-to-bumper traffic. I started taking the train a week into June. But in order to get to work on time, I had to run from Union Station to The Star, down smoggy streets, my lungs and eyes aching on arrival.

This was a month in which Toronto endured a heat wave of 30C temperatures, stifling heat accompanied by smog and public warnings of pollution levels that reportedly sent calls to emergency services soaring.

Emergency wards were also seeing the first victims of heat/smog conditions: the elderly, those with breathing disorders or cardiac problems. Some people pass out from such conditions. Others die. [1].

As the Toronto Star's Kerry Gillespie reports:

"Air pollution contributes to the deaths of 1,700 people in Toronto each year and sends 6,000 to hospital; a study has found... vehicles – from the family car to industrial equipment – are the biggest producers of air pollution in Toronto. Even though cars are getting cleaner, he pollution they cause is getting worse because there are more of them on the road and people are spending more time in them... when it comes to nitrogen dioxide, which increases with vehicle use, Toronto ranks fourth highest, just behind Los Angeles, Hong Kong and New York, the study found." [2].

Noise pollution is also a major concern. Shouted conversations are common along busy streets where the din of traffic and blaring of morons' car horns mixes with jack hammers and sirens in a LOUD assault on anyone's sense of hearing.

Breathing in polluted air, trying to cope with the noise assault, trying to make your way along congested, dust-blown, busy streets all adversely affect the health of people who spend any significant amount of time in this very polluted and noisy city.

The Greater Toronto Area's population explosion is also putting unprecedented pressure on health care services. As The Star's medical reporter, Elaine Carey observes:

"The Greater Toronto region faces a 46 per cent increase in cancer cases in the next decade and will need a massive injection of health resources to cope with it, a report says. By 2014, the region will have 33,544 new cases of cancer a year, up from 23,023 this year, because of its growing and aging population says the report by Cancer Care Ontario, obtained by the Star. The region also faces an 18 per cent increase in the number of people living with cancer." 3.

Piggish Hogtown

Toronto has borne the name Hogtown for generations. The name is originally owed to the community's historical role as a meat packing, pork processing centre with numerous abattoirs where hogs met their demise with nary a shed tear.

In recent years, Toronto's Hogtown nickname has become more derogatory (if that's possible), with current definitions of Hogtown owing more to the city's insatiable appetite for social gluttony than any prowess with pigs.

It's a big fat pig of a city (I'm sorry but it needed to be said). And it's here that bulk of major financial institutions, major corporations, even the national stock exchange, make their home. Most of the major media are here, along with most of the biggest cultural institutions. And still this big pig of a city grunts and squeals for more, more, more. More investment dollars, more government funding, more condo towers, more congestion. And more power – separate city status would make a nice desert between ongoing bouts of power gorging.

Hogtown's original historical significance hasn't entirely

disappeared however: On Stafford Street, near King Street West, the fragrant smell of pig poop wafts through the air, no doubt delighting patrons of nearby outdoor restaurant patios. The evening's entertainment: The sounds of squealing pigs being slaughtered at the Toronto Abattoirs – more commonly known as Quality Meat Packers.

Most of the local industry – such as Inglis and the Massey Ferguson farm machinery plant – has long faded from memory but the Abattoirs have been going steadily for nearly half a century, currently slaughtering 1.4-million hogs a year at a site that's been a killing field for pigs since 1915.

Still the stench inconvenience is worth it just to see the startled looks of restaurant patrons shocked by the sound of squeals as they bite into a bacon and tomato sandwich.

Too Much Garbage

As Toronto grows, it logically generates more waste. But the city has never been particularly wise or efficient or effective in disposing of its waste.

Back in the 1830s when the community numbered around 10,000 people, the citizenry dumped most of its refuse – including dead animals, manure and human waste – into the harbour, the same harbour it drew drinking water from, prompting cholera outbreaks from people drinking untreated lake water.   4.

By the 1950s, raw sewage was recognized as a problem, and by the mid-1960s, studies found up to 60,000 red sludge worms in water samples, evidence of severe sewage pollution. By the mid 1980s, testing found numerous visible contaminants along with unseen cancer-causing substances.   5.

Mercifully, Toronto has long ceased using Lake Ontario as a dump. Instead, it's overloaded its landfill sites past capacity and has turned to other communities – in northern Ontario and the American state of Michigan – to take its never-ending truckloads of waste.

This incompetence at dealing with its waste has surfaced from time to time as an election issue, most recently in the race that elected David Miller mayor.

Wasting Away

It's a recurring issue and a source of shame as nothing is ever done to resolve the issue with a long-term solution. As the Toronto Star's Ian Urquhart reports:

> "Every day, 150 trucks take the garbage from Toronto and the surrounding regions several hundred kilometres down the road to a dump in Michigan. What happens if the border is closed? It is a nightmare scenario that the provincial government would rather not contemplate. But folks in Michigan – including Governor Jennifer Granholm and the state legislature – are doing their best to keep Toronto's garbage out of their dumps... Michiganders passed their own law, due to take effect Oct. 1, which will force rigid inspections of Toronto's garbage to ensure that it does not contain recyclables or medical waste before it is dumped in a Michigan landfill... John Kerry, the Democratic presidential candidate, has already promised to do something to block Toronto's garbage "in the first 120 days of my presidency." 6.

Of course, any threat or discussion of closing borders sets Toronto politicians on edge because there is no backup plan to handle the city's garbage if the trucks can't get to Michigan. The city has the capacity to store garbage for only two days.

But when we talk about Toronto garbage, what, specifically are we referring to? According to the City of Toronto, non-recyclable items, which Torontonians throw out each year that wind up on a Michigan landfill site include 100,000 mattresses, 2.3 million square metres of carpet, 15 million large potato chip

147

bags, 10 million light bulbs, and, for those bargain-hunting garbage pickers out there: 5 million previously enjoyed toothbrushes
– some in near mint condition.

To its credit, Toronto is in fact reclaiming green space
from some of its former eyesores. Concerning the Vaughn community just north of Toronto, The Toronto Star's Gail Swainson
notes:

> "The City of Vaughn is forging ahead with an
> ambitious $19 million plan to revitalize part of the now
> defunct Keele Valley landfill site, thereby transforming
> garbage into gardens." 7.

Swainson noted the Keele Valley landfill site closed in
2003 after the neighbourhood had enough of heavy truck traffic,
seagulls and stench. Vaughn was also negotiating with Toronto to
take over the adjacent 83-hectare Avondale compost recycling
site and turn it into a recreational park complete with soccer fields
and play areas. 8.

Neglected Waterfront

Although Toronto has long ceased using its scenic harbour
as a dump site, the waterfront has been a neglected asset for
generations.

Yet, Toronto is situated on an enviable site many municipalities would kill for. It's a picturesque setting on the Lake Ontario
shoreline.

Waterfront views take in the serene waters of the lake,
made calm by the buffer of lush green Toronto islands.

But Toronto has largely squandered its enviable location.
Drab slabs of condo towers line much of the shoreline, blocking
out a view of the lake.

Old industrial buildings, some abandoned, also crowd for
space on the waterfront. And public access is severely limited.

Worse, there are very few "people places" along the shoreline where citizens can, without charge, enjoy this close proximity to the water.   9.

This is all in sharp contrast to other major cities such as Chicago, New York, San Francisco, Pittsburgh, Los Angeles, Paris and London, not to mention Sydney, Australia and Copenhagen, Denmark, both of which boast opera houses and parks on their shorelines.   10.

In contrast, Toronto's harbourfront is something of an afterthought for the city, a place that's enjoyed by wealthy sailing enthusiasts, the privileged few.

Reclaiming the Harbour

But as Toronto Star columnist Christopher Hume notes, a long history of squandered opportunities may be about to change for the better.

Commenting on yet another waterfront condominium project, Hume notes:

"Sitting on the northwest corner of Queens Quay W. and York St., the two towers (with a third on the way) of Waterclub occupy a prime site on the city's fast-changing waterfront... One also wonders about the size, width and placement of the towers, which seem designed to block the views - or what remains of them - from the city. Would Toronto not have been better served if the towers were thinner, but taller? Still, there's no question, these condos represent a big step forwarding the evolution of the waterfront. They seem intended for pedestrians as well as drivers and succeed in bringing an element of residential sophistication to an important neighbourhood that may yet reach its potential."   11.

Hume saw further reason for optimism when he took a

close look at waterfront revitalization efforts and observed:

> "Torontonians are understandably skeptical about the revitalization of the waterfront, but finally there's reason for optimism. True, it's not huge, but the glimmer of hope comes in the form of a new promenade that extends several hundred metres from York Quay to John Quay... More important, perhaps, it reveals the enormous potential of shoreline... Though much remains to be done, a new 12-metre-wide pedestrian walkway lined with trees is already in place... Still to come is a boardwalk that will reach five metres out into the lake, along with several floating piers where tour boats will dock... Also on its way is the street furniture - light fixtures, garbage cans, wooden benches - that will be installed along the promenade... Eventually, a series of beacons will illuminate the central waterfront... even in its most preliminary form; the walkway introduces an unprecedented sense of continuity, coherence and connection to the waterfront. The feelings of disruption and dislocation that characterized the lakeshore for decades have been eliminated; in their place we have a genuine waterfront precinct, fully urban yet set apart from the city. There's a long way to go, no question, but at last there's something to see, a hint of what could be..." [12].

It remains to be seen how the waterfront will evolve. Some are pushing for a 200-hectare green park and a freeze on residential development to keep the lands east of Yonge Street free of condos.

This would effectively curb the ongoing onslaught of view-blocking condo projects.

Others insist residential development is core to making the waterfront work, that it can't simply exist as a park but must be a place where many people live as well.

The conflicting visions have at times dragged the water-fronts evolution to a halt and prevented any positive steps from being taken.

That said, some worthwhile developments are getting the go-ahead.

Indeed, positive changes are also in the works for Toronto's waterfront in the form of HtO, a public park providing some greenery at Maple Leaf Quay in the city's concrete waterfront wasteland.

As the Toronto Star's Christopher Hume observes: "Designed by one of Canada's leading firms of landscape architects, Janet Rosenberg and Associates, the $7.5 million park will occupy four hectares on either side of the quay, just east of Spadina Ave." 13.

Making Lakeshore Accessible

As Hume suggests, the fall 2004-spring 2005 project comes not a moment too soon: "The lakeshore, especially the stretch from Yonge to Spadina is surprisingly inaccessible. Not only that, but much of it is also shockingly degraded either through neglect or inferior development. HtO, which will be ready for use late next year, should go a long way to changing all that... the park will reinvent the image of the urban shoreline as a man-made locale that isn't industrial, post-industrial or fake-natural." 14.

Further east on the waterfront, past a collection of view-blocking condo towers hogging the shoreline, lies a 12-acre site at the foot of the Don Roadway. It's here that a proposed $175 million commercial/residential complex is to be built with state-of-the-art film studios at its core.

The privately financed project is to eventually also feature a people-place boardwalk on these city-owned port lands. The project has the potential to transform Toronto's $1 billion film

151

industry into a multi-billion-dollar entity.

Let's hope the waterfront revitalization and improvements to the city's transportation infrastructure come to pass, and soon.

With its depressing, mind-numbing traffic congestion (Atlanta with the same population has as many as eight traffic lanes going in and out of the city; Toronto has three), dangerous levels of air pollution, unacceptable violent crime rates, sky-high cost of living and ongoing problems of poverty and homelessness, Toronto risks a growing exodus of people who have simply had all they can take.

Leaving Toronto

In fact, a steady stream of departures from people leaving Toronto has been going on for years.

The outward migration issue has attracted the attention of Bryan Levman, who heads Guidelines Advertising Ltd., one of the largest agencies serving the new home market.

In an article that appeared in The Toronto Star, Levman notes:

> "Everyone knows that Toronto's growing by leaps and bounds - an average 85,000 people every year over the last 10 years. Lost in the large immigration numbers, however, is the number of people - about 50,000 - who move out of the GTA every year… we're taking in almost 100,000 people per year from international immigration… about 24,000 annually from other provinces and about 11,000 per year from other areas of the province... The total influx is somewhere around 135,000 per year over the last 10 years, although in 2001 and 2002 we were well over 150,000… But we're also losing a significant number of people, which is why the city only grows by 85,000 annually…. It's a significant trend. From within the province, more people are leaving the GTA than set-

tling here… Were it not for the large number of new immigrants, the GTA population would actually be declining." 15.

Levman cites a number of reasons why people leave Toronto, including retirement to a less costly community, noting "Toronto just doesn't have the amenities or the ambiance that many retirees are looking for and it's too expensive for many retirement incomes." He adds:

"Urban antipathy is certainly another factor. Toronto is one of the safest cities in the world, but that's not what many residents think. The fabric of the city has changed so much in the last few decades that many yearn for a simpler, less hectic lifestyle which they find in small towns and villages of rural Ontario…Then there are the people who have opted out… these people may have decided that the hectic pace of the city, the pollution and the crowding are unbearable and have chosen to make a major change in their lives… urban antipathy, burnout and desire for clean air and proximity to nature, etc. - are increasing all the time, as life in the fast lane seems to get faster and faster every year." 16.

Toronto rules Canada

Toronto is by far Canada's most influential city and it is no exaggeration to state that this city effectively rules Canadian culture, politics and social agenda.

With a growing number of Toronto politicians making the claim that the city is being short-changed in terms of public funding from upper levels of government.

And, with various city denizens advocating "city state" status for Toronto and a louder voice in provincial and federal politics, alarm bells are ringing.

Those bells are being rung by smaller centres across Canada who fear Toronto will use its size to dominate the public agenda to an even greater extent than it already does.

Peter McQuaid, former chief of staff to Prince Edward Island Premier Pat Binns, has voiced strong concerns about Toronto's tightening stranglehold on the country, a hold that threatens to become tighter still with the big city agenda advocated by Toronto.

"It will change the whole structure of the country," McQuaid told the Toronto Star's Kelly Toughill:

> "If the cities want to sit at the table with the federal government and the provinces, we will end up with a tripartite system and places like P.E.I. and the Maritimes will get lost. It boils down to where we are going to have a debate about confederation, or will this be done through the back door?" 17.

And we've already heard from the Ottawa Citizen with its charge that Toronto is the "whine capital" of Canada for demanding virtual city state status. To his credit however, Mayor David Miller has broadened his pitch and now argues all major Canadian cities – not just Toronto – need more autonomy over their affairs.

Cash Needed for Cure

But solving Toronto's liveability problems may ultimately mean putting more cash and power into the hands of local politicians and authorities closest to the urban front lines.

Nor can Toronto be fairly compared in all matters to much smaller centres.

Former Toronto Star publisher John Honderich makes a salient point when he argues Toronto has needs that are markedly different than those of smaller centres with less congestion, immigration, overcrowding, traffic, crime and housing concerns.

And, concerning the sharing of fuel taxes, Honderich says sharing is a great idea – but it must be done fairly based on the right criteria. He observed:

> "Queen's Park has promised to hand over several cents per litre to municipalities to lessen the burden of financing public transit. If the formula for sharing were based on population, Toronto would get slightly more than 20 per cent of the total. But if it's based on ridership of public transit, that figure shoots up to more than 60 per cent. And this gap is worth tens of millions of dollars." 18.

I can sympathize with non-Torontonians who feel this very influential and wealthy city is simply whining for more power. And I can see why such separate status efforts irk people and may make them hate Toronto.

Toronto Needs Power

However, in all honesty, I believe there's a compelling case to be made for granting Toronto more power and money to address its various problems and efficiently resolve them.

Indeed, a strong argument can be made that Toronto is being badly short-changed by upper levels of government and is being denied the basic tools it needs to properly function as Canada's largest city.

Jane Jacobs, the U.S.-born, Toronto-based author of several books on how urban centres work, finds Toronto has been forced to cut back its spending on programs and incur budget shortfalls for no good reason.

Jacobs asserts such spending cuts are not due to economic necessity but are instead owed to a tight-fisted reluctance of upper levels of government to give back to the city a reasonable amount of the tax revenue it raises for federal and provincial governments. 19.

In essence, Toronto is a rich city that has been placed in a state of artificial poverty by big governments that waste these tax dollars while public transit, the education system and homeless people do without.

Financial Straitjacket

Jacobs warns that this deliberately imposed financial straitjacket is making it difficult for Toronto to deal with such compelling issues as diminished opportunities in education - now treated like a business with little emphasis on the joy and value of learning - and the loss of a sense of community. [20.]

She dismisses the neoconservative belief that education funding cutbacks are necessary because public education is expense, asserting that "life is expensive." [21.]

And what does society gain by putting young people through academic factories that depersonalize education, offer little direct professorial contact and leave graduates deep in debt?

Failure to connect new generations to society, culture and history can result in a forgetting of who and what we are and what we value, resulting in a new Dark Age, Jacobs warns. [22.]

Jacobs says society's short-sighted, cost-cutting approach can have far-reaching consequences. As an example, she cites last year's SARS outbreak in Toronto:

> "There weren't enough nurses... The idea was there were too many and we could save money by stripping these down. But you can't take the rock-bottom needs and expect they will take care of all kinds of emergencies; they won't do it." [23.]

Toronto Star columnist Royson James laments the city's slide into a degree of urban decay and neglect:

"Visitors and returning Torontonians can't help but notice the unraveling of the city's fabric right in front of them on city streets. The homeless. The beggars. The drug- and alcohol-addled sleeping on subway grates. The despair. The filthy streets mocking the city's once-unassailable image as a city of order and cleanliness. Potholes. Weeds. And this despoiling, what Jacobs calls "Toronto's desperate cheeseparing," is not a result of economic hardship or a failure to generate riches for the federal and provincial coffers. Toronto residents and businesses pay some $21 billion in taxes to all governments, but only about 5 per cent goes to the city. The net outflow hovers around $9 billion." 24.

But James also believes there are signs a determined effort to turn things around may be underway:

"This place on the shores of Lake Ontario was once an urbanist's dream, a city that worked, a place of innovation, of diversity, of strong local democracy. It languishes now, but there are signs of a primal stirring. A new mayor, David Miller, understands all that Jacobs speaks of, feels it in his bones, really. Citizens are re-engaging in civic pursuits, as seen in the response to the first citywide cleanup day. All we need is for one of the pillars of our culture, our tax-holding provincial and federal governments, to catch the vision, or at least face the fear of a civic culture facing an artificial dead end, one it can forestall." 25.

Although Toronto can come across as pompous and self-aggrandizing in its demands, it's an inescapable fact that to fully live up to its potential and achieve new heights, Toronto does indeed need to have more control over its destiny – as annoying as that may be to the rest of us.

Alan Broadbent, chairman of Avana Capital Corp. and a member of the Toronto City Summit Alliance, notes bashing Toronto doesn't change the fact that this city has unique needs that differ broadly from those of smaller towns and communities.

Arguing that Toronto should be entitled to meet directly with senior levels of government, Broadbent observes:

> "We live with a system of government that might have made some sense in 1867, at the time of Confederation, but makes less sense today... We know that our large cities generate the bulk of the wealth created in Canada, a far cry from 1867 when the hinterland produced wealth from furs, lumber, fish, mines and farm produce. Now such extractive industries account for fewer than 3 per cent of Canada's economic production." [26.]

"Instead," Broadbent adds, "it is the urban-based wealth creation that exports capital to the rest of the country via the provincial and federal governments. The Toronto region alone sends approximately $15-billion a year more than it receives." [27.]

Toronto is the capital of Ontario. Think about what that means: Toronto is the decision-making centre for Canada's most populous province.

Costly Power Brownouts/Blackouts

So how are they doing? In many areas, poorly. On the energy front in particular, poor planning has resulted in higher than necessary energy costs being passed on to the consumer - adding to the already overly high cost of living in Toronto.

Ontario is burdened with rising energy costs, electrical power outages and breakdowns, mothballed nuclear plants and electricity shortages resulting in numerous 'brownouts' and pleas from Queen's Park - the provincial capital in Toronto - to use less energy.

This is the same Queen's Park that previously told us to use lots of electricity.

In its 'wisdom', the Toronto-based provincial capital has privatized electricity, thus ensuring its prices will rise and rise to ensure profits for its private shareholders.

So why don't we buy from neighbouring provinces while waiting for our own investments in new power facilities to come on stream?

First, we don't have any new power generating facilities coming on stream and our mothballed nuclear plants remain idle with no plans to revive them.

As for buying power from neighbouring provinces, the logical choice would be Quebec, which produces a huge surplus of power and still has plenty of it left after selling it to Canadians in Quebec.

$20 billion to Decommission Reactors

Hydro expert Tony O'Donohue says it will cost as much as $20-billion to decommission the aging nuclear reactors the province already owns and he strongly suggests Ontario should replace nuclear stations with more hydro-electric plants as Quebec has done.   28.

O'Donohue adds that there is enough potential power generation from Ontario's maze of major rivers to more than replace any need for nuclear power.

He notes a 1982 Ontario Hydro report stated that the utility was producing only one-third of its potential hydro-electric output, but "the report was quietly shelved by a province determined to move deeper into the fatally flawed nuclear program."   29.

O'Donohue adds: "In the 22 years since the report was released, nothing has been done to add to our hydro power, but the provincial taxpayer is in hock for $38-billion for its disastrous nuclear adventure... And, electricity prices to Quebec residential users are about half the price Ontario users pay." 30.

He says it will take 15-20 years to plan and build and electrical energy system for the province - assuming the politicians have the will to do so - and many more blackouts can be expected in the meantime.

Observing that no funds have been set aside for the inevitable decommissioning of Ontario's aging nuclear power plants, O'Donohue notes:

"If we ignore the full (and dire) implications of decommissioning, the aging Pickering reactors will soon run out of steam, and we will face the prospect of having the decaying radioactive hulk... indefinitely." 31.

The Toronto-based provincial government appears to have come up short when it comes to properly planning the decommissioning of aging nuclear plants.

Addressing Urban Sprawl

But to its credit, the City of Toronto is addressing problems on a few fronts, including the major issue of urban sprawl that eliminates farmland, adds to already insufferable traffic congestion levels and erases many of the few natural areas we have left.

Toronto is also taking measures to control urban sprawl via an initiative from Queen's Park that recognizes Toronto's explosive population and traffic growth are expected to continue at a record pace that will surpass the ability of existing infrastructure to accommodate such growth.

For example, the plan anticipates already-long commuting times will increase by 45 percent in years to come while pollution and population growth are expected to soar.

While noting support for an ambitious corrective plan

limiting growth to 26 designated centres may not materialize, Kerry Gillespie of the Toronto Star observes:

> "The province wants to get rid of traffic conges-
> tion, expand transit everywhere in the GTA, save
> farmland and make the Greater Golden Horseshoe an
> international economic engine." 32.

While noting the 30-year growth plan 'Places to Grow: Better Choices. Brighter Future' document is a bit short on specifics, The Spectator's Bill Dunphy notes the plan, if finalized and implemented, could potentially dramatically change Toronto for the better.

The Good Old Days

As Dunphy points out, the plan calls for a number of changes that recall an earlier, idealistic era:

> "More transit, fewer cars; more density, fewer
> subdivisions; putting people where the services are,
> rather than running services to where someone's
> gobbled up some cheap land; rewarding developers
> who work embroiders the social fabric, penalizing those
> who rip it apart - these ideas were building blocks of an
> activist coalition that changed the face of Toronto... And
> now, these same ideas provide the underpinning for the
> province's new 30-year growth plan..." 33.

Much of Toronto is asphalt and concrete.

On my short run each day from Union Station to The Toronto Star at One Yonge, my feet are continually hitting hard pavement as I cut through crowded parking lots and dash across busy, dust-blown roadways filled with noise and fast-moving traffic. It's a run to be enduring not enjoyed.

Unlike other major cities where outdoor cafes and patio restaurants and parkettes with benches dominate the street-level landscape, Toronto only has pockets of truly livable areas in an overall sea of pavement.

Can't See the Forest

Coupled with the need to preserve outlying natural spaces, Toronto also needs to make the inner city experience more inviting. Trees, gardens and benches can make a huge difference in transforming those parts of the city that a currently little more than a concrete jungle. As Christopher Hume notes:

"Perhaps because of our climactic challenges, Torontonians have never developed a genuine street culture, as have many cities in Europe and Canada - think of Montreal or Vancouver. Even the now ubiquitous outdoor cafe has only been a feature of Toronto life since the 1960s; before then the idea of using the sidewalks for anything more than walking was deemed unseemly, if not downright suspicious. But as Toronto has grown more multicultural, so have attitudes towards its streets. Finally we are starting to understand that the public realm is the chief glory of this city, or any, for that matter. Though we'll never be able to compete with Paris, New York or Barcelona, benches are as accurate an indicator as any of how we're doing. Parks are an obvious starting place; even in the upright days of Toronto the Good, citizens were allowed to sit on park benches. But they were expected to keep their legs crossed, of course, and avoid eye contact with passersby or anyone sitting beside them. Though it wasn't much, it was a beginning. Today, parks are still places to go to find public seating. The options range wildly from the traditional dark green wooden benches to the edgy circular seats in Yorkville Park." [34.]

Hume is also concerned about the lack of attention

given to the natural benefits provided by trees. Too many trees, he argues, are being lost to concrete and pavement. He notes:

"If a tree falls in the city, does anybody hear? The answer, it seems, is no. But given the rate at which they are disappearing from the streets of Toronto, our ears should be ringing. "The urban forest is in serious decline," declares Toronto's official tree advocate, Deputy Mayor Joe Pantalone. "In 1992, 22 per cent of the old city of Toronto was covered by tree canopy," he explains. "Now we're down to 16 per cent. The reason is that our community doesn't value trees as much as it should. We don't have enough trees and we don't plant enough trees." There are still many trees in Toronto, cleaning the air, providing shade and generally acting as the lungs of the city. But many are poor, stunted specimens that barely look like trees and never will. Planted in cramped quarters filled with bad soil and attacked by salt, they don't stand a chance. What a shame Trees aren't just good for people, they're great for cities. Indeed, trees are much more than carbon-dioxide filters. In the most sophisticated cities - London, Paris - they form part of the urban architecture. They are not just plants but elements of the landscape used to define space, separate and connect it. Perhaps no one understands the potential of trees better than the French. Every city, town and village appears to have an active tree-planting and maintenance program... In Paris, on the Champs Elysees... trees transform what is essentially an eight-lane highway into one of the world's most visited pedestrian precincts. Walkers are protected by three rows of trees along each side of the street... trees are an indispensable aspect of the urban fabric, as important as sidewalks, roads or buildings..." 35.

Toronto proper covers more than 640 square kilometres and boasts 1,500 parks with more than 8,000 square kilometres of parkland. That's impressive.

But contact with nature is often simply not there in much of the city, despite huge tracts of parkland tucked away here and there.

What's needed is for Toronto to introduce more green space – even small parks – and trees to its many user-unfriendly city streets.

Trees also help break up and partly muffle traffic noise.

Judicious planting of trees and floral patches can help change the pedestrian experience from a hateful endurance test to an enjoyable stroll – provided the political will is there to make this transformation happen.

If not, the city's streets will continue to be avenues of resentment that provide another reason to hate Toronto.

Congestion, not just traffic but people, is another factor making Toronto and unliveable city.

We've mentioned that 100,000 or more people pour into this city every year.

If you think about it for a moment, Toronto is absorbing the population of a mid-sized city, growing by size of mid-sized city every year, year after year.

And many of the newcomers don't speak the language. In a city of strangers, the cacophony of competing shouts in foreign languages makes the city feel stranger still.

Although the economic contribution ambitious immigrants make to Toronto outweighs such adjustments, the initial impact can still be jarring.

It's easy to feel lost in Toronto, to feel as though you don't belong here.

The Toronto Star's Libby Stephens recently compiled a list of observations from newsroom colleagues, and I'll include just a few of them here.

You know you live in Toronto when:

"You make more than $300,000 a year and still can't afford a house; you take public transit and are shocked at two people carrying on a conversation – in English; you've been to a baby shower that has two mothers and a sperm donor; your car insurance costs as much as your house payment; a really great parking space can move you to tears; gas usually costs 74 to 78 cents per litre – more than anywhere else in Canada; it's barely snowing and there's a report on every news station about 'Storm Watch 2004'; you pass an elementary school playground and the children are all busy with their cell-phones or pagers; and, it's barely sprinkling rain outside, so you leave for work an hour early to avoid all the weather-related accidents." 36.

It's interesting that this humorous list started with the high cost of real estate, followed with the housing affordability issue and included the chatter of others in foreign tongues.

These are all things that set Toronto apart from many other Canadian urban centres. They're also things that can make you feel as though you don't belong.

How can you feel at home in a city where you can't afford a home and have trouble communicating with the neighbours?

To a degree, many Canadians have difficulty relating to Toronto. And this too is a source of resentment, and yet another reason why so many people hate Toronto.

"Toronto is much, much more than Canada's largest city. It's the cultural centre that defines Canadian culture. It's the creator of great music, films and literature. It's the nation's economic, financial, cultural, performing arts and professional sports heartland. It's the home of great works of art and architecture. It's the height of Canadian civilization."
Michael B. Davie, author, *Why Everybody Hates Toronto*.

"I lived in Vancouver during the '80s and I have fond memories of the sea wall around Stanley Park and the ferry to Salt Spring Island and some splendid people, but when I returned to Toronto I felt I was going, culturally speaking, from a high school to a university."
Philip Marchand, Toronto Star writer/ book reviewer.

10

The Main Reason

At this point we've explored many of the reasons everybody – or at least an awful lot of people – hate Toronto. These reasons include: crazy drivers, traffic congestion, exorbitant parking rates, sky-high housing costs, overcrowded streets, punitive tuition rates, and overly serious and condescending business attitudes, a squandering of civic assets, a pervasive and judgemental political correctness, and growing problems with violent crime, poverty and homelessness. To varying degrees, all of these factors have some validity and each of these reasons is supported by evidence. Each reason contributes to overall feelings of dislike towards Toronto.

Now let's examine the leading reason, the number one reason, the main reason that often takes the role of hidden, underlying subtext beneath the more-often-stated reasons. It's a reason that's rarely ever stated by anyone. Yet this reason more than any other is why so many people really profess to hate Toronto.

This main reason, simply put, is envy.

For all of its many problems, Toronto is, without question, a truly remarkable city. And that's a major source of envy for the rest of us who can never aspire to reach Toronto's heights.

Even some of Toronto's problems inspire envy. Toronto is grappling with problems of constant construction development and a population explosion. Most cities have great difficulty attracting any investment and struggle to maintain shrinking populations. They'd love to have to deal with an array of major investors and an expanding consumer base – not to mention an ever-expanding tax base.

Of course it doesn't hurt that Toronto is the capital of Ontario, the most populous of provinces. But government spending and prestige don't tell the full story of Toronto's success" Ottawa is the capital of the whole country – and it's just a fraction of the size and importance of Toronto.

Toronto is much, much more than Canada's largest city. It's the cultural centre that defines Canadian culture. It's the creator of great music, films and literature. It's the nation's economic, financial, cultural, performing arts and professional sports heartland. It's the home of great works of art and architecture. It's the height of Canadian civilization.

Yes, there are many days when I'm gagging on polluted air, inching my way through bumper-to-bumper traffic jams to take on a heavy stress-load that I ask myself why I'm doing this. Wouldn't I be happier in a smaller centre, working for a smaller newspaper, living a smaller life?

But there are also days when I approach this dynamic city and its bold skyline with a sense of adventure and awe. I have to remind myself that I'm actually living the Toronto experience, tasting and savouring life in one of the world's great cities. The Big Time in the Big Smoke. There's a feeling of excitement, of achievement, of being more than I was before. I often feel privileged and fortunate to be a part of it all. Toronto is our Paris, our London, our New York. Toronto is above all Toronto, a truly awesome city.

How does one effectively describe the Toronto experience? The Toronto Star's Philip Marchand, quite possibly the greatest book-reviewer in the world, observes:

"I lived in Vancouver during the '80s and I have fond memories of the sea wall around Stanley Park and the ferry to Salt Spring Island and some splendid people, but when I returned to Toronto I felt I was going, culturally speaking, from a high school to a university." 1.

Marchand cites the density of Toronto's media environment – including a wealth of television and radio stations and five daily newspapers – plus the city's multicultural diversity as being "two things (that) make Toronto, despite all its problems, a place of extraordinary sophistication and energy." 2.

Indeed, the whole of Toronto is much greater than the sum of its parts. It's a vibrant centre for literary, journalistic, television and film industry creativity. It's the financial capital of Canada – home to the big banks, the Toronto Stock Exchange, a wealth of financial planners and investors – and it's one of the world's great financial centres.

Surprisingly, despite its many towering buildings and its reputation (deserved in some parts of the city) as a concrete jungle, much of Toronto is actually a lush green city filled with parks.

As the Toronto Star's Andrew Mills observes: "It's been called the city of ravines, the city of trees, the city of forgotten rivers. But when you think about it for a moment, Toronto and the region around it is really a city of parks. Like long green fingers that interrupt the urban sprawl or giant breaths of fresh air amid the soupy exhaust, this region's parks give it life." 3.

Mills notes that surveys of Toronto's parks show most are very well maintained and inviting. But vigilance is necessary to ensure Toronto's urban escapes remain lush and spotless: The population has exploded in size, while park maintenance budgets have been reduced, placing a strain on the natural amenities and park-related facilities in Toronto's 1,470 parks and the hundreds of additional parks in the surrounding region. 4.

Most of the nation's biggest newspapers and magazines are headquartered in Toronto.

So are all of the biggest publishing houses and most of the biggest printing companies. In fact, even by world standards, Toronto is a major publishing centre.

Toronto's cultural role on the publishing front is evident in its former Word On The Street books festival in which dozens of publishers and authors present their works to a voracious reading public.

The annual events drew as many as 170,000 people. In 2004, the event was renamed Word In The Park and relocated to the spacious provincial legislative grounds of Queen's Park – where it drew crowds of more than 200,000 along with enormous media attention.

Huge crowds also turn out for the annual Science Fiction/Fantasy book fairs that draw every increasing attendance levels to this Toronto cultural attraction.

Indeed, Toronto is also increasing the size and scope of its role as the leading centre of culture in Canada.

In addition to such cultural institutions as the Royal Ontario Museum, the Art Gallery of Ontario, The Royal Conservatory of Music, Ontario Place, The Science Centre, and the National Ballet School, not to mention an array of performing arts venues such as The Royal Alexander Theatre, Pantages Theatre, Molson Amphitheatre, Air Canada Centre, Hummingbird Centre, Skydome and countless smaller venues, Toronto, in 2004, was in the process of building the state-of-the-art Four Seasons Centre for the Performing Arts, more commonly known as the new opera house. This is to be a new home for the National Ballet of Canada, live opera performances and other performing arts.

Toronto routinely draws major stars during its annual indications of famous Canadians (many from Toronto) for Canada's

Walk of Fame. As well, the city's numerous, constantly fully booked, sports and entertainment venues guarantee a constant, shifting population of stars visiting or residing in Toronto (Canadian singer-songwriters Gordon Lightfoot and Murray McLauchlan, and the band members of Blue Rodeo, The Cowboy Junkies, Parachute Club, Rush and many other bands all reside here, as does American recording artist Prince and a host of Canadian and international actors, entertainers and sports figures).

Adding to Toronto's growing reputation as a magnet for the stars, is its international presence as Hollywood North – a major centre for the filming and production of motion pictures.

On any given day in Toronto there's usually a Hollywood blockbuster being shot on location on city streets, with Robert DeNiro or Kevin Bacon or Russell Crowe or any of a number of other superstars wandering city streets, dining in local posh restaurants and generally making themselves at home in one of the world's great cities.

Hollywood itself isn't always that thrilled with the success of Hollywood North. Some in the California movie industry have complained about the number of American movies being shot in Toronto instead of the United States (such sniping is a sure indicator of real success) and have dubbed Toronto as the capital of runaway film production.

Movie stars aren't your cup of tea? You can also catch live music performances by major artists at the Skydome, Molson Amphitheatre, Exhibition Stadium, Varsity Stadium, the Hummingbird Centre, and numerous other venues large or intimate throughout the city.

As if that's not enough, Toronto also hosted SARSstock, a life concert experience intended to counteract the negative publicity surrounding the city's brief SARS health crisis.

Performers included The Rolling Stones, AC/DC, Rush, the Guess Who, Sam Roberts, Sarah Harmer and many others.

Movies are your cup of tea? In that case, you'll no doubt

be impressed that Toronto host one of the world's top film festivals. The renowned Toronto Film Festival annually attracts more than 400 stars and directors, so many in fact that regular folk can seem like a minority as they compete for seats in posh restaurants.

Fortunately the city has more than 8,000 dining establishments ranging from fast-food outlets to stately establishments.

As Toronto Star movie critic Peter Howell notes, the 2004 Toronto Film Festival featured a bevy of stars, including Canadians Sarah Polley, Gordon Pinsent, Martin Short, Brendan Fraser, Callum Keith Rennie, Maury Chaykin Paul Gross, Don McKellar, Eric McCormack and Mike Myers, along with such other international stars as Claire Danes, Al Pacino, Sean Penn, Kevin Spacey, Dustin Hoffman, Annette Bening, Warren Beatty, Mandy Moore, Charlize Teron, Nick Nolte, Danny Glover, Sigourney Weaver, Jennifer Tilly, Helen Hunt, Susan Sarandon, Gabriel Byrne and many more, "rivalling the Cannes Film Festival and the Academy Awards for international celebrity dazzle." [5.]

Howell also notes that Toronto's reputation and ability to successfully host such events has resulted in numerous world premieres of films from returning directors and producers. [6.]

And the stars can't get enough of the local restaurants and scenery.
In addition to those stars already mentioned, such popular actors as Orlando Bloom have been spotted in the entertainment district, along with actors Mark Wahlberg, Viggo Mortensen, Jamie Foxx, Kate Bosworth, and Matt Dillon, directors such as Norman Jewison and rock stars along the lines of Sass Jordan, Daniel Lanois, Carole Pope – all Canadians – and Peter Gabriel (the more celebrity names I include, the more space I fill up in this book. Interesting).

Toronto also boasts an array of popular night clubs, restaurants, bars, pubs, jazz clubs and other hot spots to see and be seen.

Queen Street West is home to numerous such establishments, including the legendary Drake Hotel, a haunt of Nick Nolte and something of a magnet to literary, film and performing arts icons, people like Sean Connery, Harrison Ford, Neil Young and Joni Mitchell, though not necessarily Sean Connery, Harrison Ford, Neil Young and Joni Mitchell themselves – but people who are, in fact, like them.

This joint is always buzzing with the beautiful people, even when it's quiet in the city's other sought-after establishments, such as the Windsor Arms favoured by Jeremy Irons or the lounge of the Four Seasons hotel (a favourite hangout of Al Pacino).

Other hotspots include Flow (formerly the Movenpick) in Yorkville; Canoe; the Rosewater Supper Club on Toronto Street (which draws the likes of Woody Harrelson, Sean Penn, Pierce Brosnan and Dustin Hoffman whenever they're in town); Ciro's; Michelle's Brasserie; The Cloak And Dagger; Cobalt, Local 4; and, the Bistro 990 on Bay Street, a dining destination of choice for Robert DeNiro, Meg Ryan, Nick Nolte and other major movie stars. Oh, and there's also the Opus, Smokeless Joe; The Esplanade Bier Markt; Castro's Lounge; The Only Café; Beerbistro; Allen's; the Lobby (a Jason Lewis haunt), Sassafraz (Tom Cruise, Billy Zane, Maria Bello and Will Smith dined there) YYZ (a Chris Noth hot spot) and the Courthouse – a favourite of Brendan Fraser, Matt Dillon, Ryan Phillippe and Sandra Bullock – and the list goes on and on and on.

Canada's Walk of Fame has an impressive array of nearly 100 Canadian inductees including a host of actors and directors from the legendary earliest years of the silver screen. From the Toronto area itself we have such Walk of Fame entertainment industry giants as Christopher Plummer, Lorne Michaels, Wayne & Shuster, Jim Carrey, John Candy, David Cronenberg, Norman Jewison and Mike Myers.

Famous Toronto recording artists on the Walk include Neil Young, John Kay and Steppenwolf, Rush, Glenn Gould and

Robbie Robertson.

Comic actor Jim Carrey recently accepted his Canada's Walk of Fame honours in 2004, along with fellow 2004 inductees, who also boast a wealth of Canadian talent. They include: Film director Denys Arcand, actors Shirley Douglas and Helen Shaver, legendary rock band John Kay and Steppenwolf, jazz singer-pianist Diana Krall and hockey great Mario Lemieux.

Also honoured at the same event were legendary, Hollywood-shaping Canadians of the distant past, including movie moguls Louis B. Mayer, Mack Sennett and Jack Warner (Warner Bros) and silver screen actresses Mary Pickford and the recently departed Fay Wray of King Kong fame.

All of the Walk of Fame inductions draw crowds of major stars, friends of stars (who are often stars themselves) and throngs of fans.

In Toronto, you can practically trip over celebrities. One Toronto Star colleague of mine recalls waiting in line at a coffee shop and noticing that the baseball-cap-wearing guy in front of him looked like George Clooney – because it was George Clooney.

The celebrities are now a population unto themselves.

If Toronto draws any more celebrities, there's the likelihood the city will invoke its time-honoured tradition of ghettoizing them into a special-needs minority group, subject to the usual government subsidies, affirmative action hiring policies and politically correct overblown platitudes about their contribution to our society.

And speaking of people making a contribution to our society (clever segue no?), Toronto leads the nation in devising, introducing and maintaining programs aimed at helping troubled youth find work and make a real contribution to the community.

In recent months and years, Toronto has introduced a number of innovative programs aimed at providing employment for youth who might otherwise remain unemployed for a very long time. Simply put, the youth go from being a drag on the system to being a contributor.

Describing a food services sector program, the Toronto Star's Christian Cotroneo reports:

"They may be a long way from reaching their dreams, but before arriving here, dreams were a luxury they could ill afford. This cozy, wedge-shaped restaurant in Toronto's west end culls its staff from the ranks of Toronto's homeless and at-risk youth... The restaurant is owned by All-A-Board youth Ventures inc., which offers jobs to at-risk youth – and a chance to build a future... Despite having scarce experience in the restaurant industry when they arrive, about 85 per cent of employees stay at least a year before moving on to other jobs." [7]

Another program, in the crime-drenched Malvern area of Toronto's Scarborough community offers five-week courses at Centennial College free of charge to troubled, at-risk youth.

Describing the Malvern area home of 70 recent graduates of these courses, Toronto Star columnist Royson James noted: "It looks like Anywhere, Suburbia, but one in three here is younger than 21. Almost half are newcomers, having arrived since 1991. And following a recent wave of gang-style shootings, (Toronto Mayor David) Miller named Malvern one of three city neighbourhoods to warrant special attention and help from his Community Safety Plan... The mayor's initiative was launched exactly six months ago to present an alternative to the traditional crime-fighting methods of increased enforcement followed by incarceration, leading to more alienation, a permanent underclass and more outcasts... to provide summer jobs in the target areas and to offer free summer classes in the trades." [8]

Toronto deserves full marks for not giving up on its troubled youth, for realizing that youth truly represent the future and that it only makes good sense to cultivate tomorrow's leaders

– including world leaders.

The Toronto Star's Angus Loten provides an example of this approach when he explains: "The World Youth Centre, a pilot project with the University of Toronto, has brought together 18 young people from around the world... to help implement their community development ideas, such as AIDS education in India or cultural connections in rural Quebec. Daily workshops teach fund-raising, promotion and project management, among other skills." 9.

Of course, in addition to innovative youth/education programs, hard-working citizens and an abundance of parkland, Toronto also boasts some wonderful world attractions including the CN Tower.

Phallic symbol observations aside, the CN Tower has defined the city's distinctive and unique skyline since it opened in 1976. Rivalling gut-wrenching amusement park rides, the tower's elevator will shoot you up to the first level, 114 metres in the air, in less than a minute.

But that's only about 20 per cent of the heights you can hit. A second elevator ride will take you up another 33 floors where breathtaking views of Toronto, Niagara Falls, Lake Ontario and Rochester are waiting.

No wonder the CN Tower attracts more than 2 million visitors every year. Be warned thought, parking is very costly and going to the top of the tower can set you back nearly $30 per person. 10.

Most of Toronto's other major attractions are more reasonably priced in the $10 to $13 range for adults and younger kids often get in free.

The Hockey Hall of Fame is well worth a visit. Here, you can touch the legendary Stanley Cup, see the net that caught The Great One Wayne Gretzky's 802nd goal, and take in the Legends tribute video.

This is Hockey Heaven at its finest (although a suitable

use for Maple Leaf Gardens must still be found – a grocery store just doesn't cut it, even if the frozen meat-pies are as hard as hockey pucks).

Ontario Place is a kid's paradise, complete with its Soak City water park, midway and plenty of water – this is a waterfront park that really works.

The Ontario Science Centre is also a major kid's attraction that appeals to adults as well. Here you can examine coral reefs, watch movies or explore the mysteries of outer space. And be sure to check out whatever's playing on the giant IMAX movie screen.

Casa Loma is a wonderful, magical castle, the former home of financier Sir Henry Pellatt and it's his tribute to an age of grand living. The 98-room hill-top mansion has secret passageways and an underground tunnel. Marvel at the vast conservatory with Italian marble floors and lose yourself in the elegant gardens.

The Art Gallery of Ontario features a superb collection of works by The Group of Seven, outstanding Henry Moore sculptures and impressive paintings by famous American and European artists such as Turner, Whistler and Monet.

Royal Ontario Museum attractions cover prehistoric to present times and include Native Indian totem poles and architecture throughout the ages including Italian Renaissance, neo-classical, Victorian and Art Deco. The museum recently underwent a multi-million renovation and it remains one of the finest such institutions of its kind anywhere.

Just strolling through mid-town Toronto is often enough to bring you face to face with some of Hollywood's biggest stars, along with major rock musicians, artists, writers and athletes. Russell Crowe hangs out in Toronto. Prince lives here.

A bevy of other stars frequently visit and their presence often graces two-page spreads in the Toronto Star on a regular basis. Many of these stars are here shooting movies in "Hollywood North," and can be found shopping in local stores, dining in

Toronto restaurants and strolling the city's many fascinating streets. Toronto has become the place to see and be seen and be a part of the scene.

Toronto's more interesting streets include Queen Street, a major thoroughfare that has evolved into one long strip/show-case of coffee shops, art galleries, restaurants, bars, nightclubs and entertainment hot spots.

It's also where you'll find a Mecca for entertainment in the big brick building that houses CITY TV, Much Music, Much More Music and several specialty cable TV channels. Many of today's top bands and entertainment acts – including the Parachute Club – cut their teeth performing in bars along Queen. It was also the street that hosted Word On The Street until the event was moved to Queen's Park in 2004, and it remains an artistic community with more than its share of prominent writers.

Toronto also seems destined to attain an even greater share of the movie industry, which already invests about $1 billion per year in this city.

In fact, the city is currently redefining its role as Hollywood North: The proposed $170 million Toronto Film Studios Inc. movie studio to be built on city-owned port lands would feature a waterfront hotel, 13 state-of-the-art sound stages and an Olympic-sized pool featuring a false bottom that could be used to film underwater scenes. The development also calls for seven production offices along with restaurants and shops.

And that's just a small sample of the mega-projects and investment dollars pouring into Toronto.

Billionaire businessman Donald Trump is building a huge commercial tower and skyscrapers continue to spring up throughout this city that never seems to stop growing.

There's a raw human energy that infuses Toronto on a daily basis. This is THE city, the city that routinely goes above and beyond anything attempted in the past, the city that forges – and helps define – Canada's future, the city that represents to the entire world just how successful – on social, economic and cultural fronts – a community can be. Simply put, Toronto is where it's all happening.

And there's a sense in the air in Toronto that anything and everything is possible, no matter how far-fetched the initial thought may seem (back to back World Series championship titles for example).

Yes, some dreams are shattered, but many more come true, and Toronto is one of the few cities anywhere that is so rich in potential.

Here, you have the opportunity to achieve success in any field you can think of.

The Toronto experience is exciting, fast-paced, exhilarating and potentially very rewarding.

And what of Torontonians themselves? Yes, they've been described by many as workaholics.

Such generalities aside, the flip side of the workaholic coin is that they are simply dedicated hard-working people who pride themselves in how much they can achieve and contribute rather than how much they can take back.

Torontonians are tireless, thoroughbred workers and entrepreneurs, leading the way in a fast-paced environment that always sets higher and higher benchmarks for success.

They set the standards. They define success.

They marry compassion with commerce. They lead the way for an entire nation to follow.

Torontonians are on the cutting edge. They're innovative, creative, brilliant, analytical, hard-driving achievers, conquering life's challenges and bolding going where few others dare.

If only they weren't so damn ugly…

Why Everybody Hates Toronto
Bibliographical Information/Notes

Notes for Chapter One
It's True: Everybody Hates Toronto

1. Michael B. Davie, 'Same-sex couples fight for the right to legal marriages. Court cases may take years' The Toronto Star, pg. K3, June 20/2002

2. Vinay Menon, 'Our exclusive guide to Hogtown survival' The Toronto Star, pg. J3, September 11, 2004.

3. Philip Marchand, 'Toronto the Ignored. Literati leave Big Smoke out in the cold', Toronto Star, November 23, 2002. pg. J4.

4. IBID

5. IBID

6. IBID

7. William Burrill, Hemingway: The Toronto Years, Toronto: Doubleday Canada Limited, 1994. pg. 152.

8. IBID

9. Editorial 'Toronto, the whine capital of Canada', The Ottawa Citizen, August 24, 2004, pg. A14.

10. IBID.

11. IBID.

12. IBID.

Notes for Chapter Three
Driving us crazy

1. Bob Mitchell, 'Motorists driven to distraction' The Toronto Star, pg. B2, May 25, 2004.
2. IBID. 3. IBID. 4. IBID. 5. IBID. 6. IBID.
7. Editorial:'On testing drivers' The Toronto Star, pg. F6, April 3, 2004.
8. Angus Loten and Frank Calleja, 'Cyclist arrives first in rush-hour traffic challenge' The Toronto Star, pg. E1, July 16, 2004.
9. Evangeline Moffat, 'Should I stay or should I GO? The Inaccessible City' The Toronto Star, pg. B3, May 9, 2004.
10. IBID.
11. Kevin McGran, 'T.O. tops in parking fees' The Toronto Star, pg. B1, July 29, 2004.

Notes for Chapter Four
Thank God it's Monday

1. Books, 'Why are we running all the time, anyway?' The Toronto Star, pg. D12, May 30, 2004.
2. Greg Bonnell, Canadian Press, 'Unplug your holiday. Just let the office take care of itself' The Toronto Star, pg. E7, August 9, 2004.
3. Judy Gerstel, 'Take off and turn it off' The Toronto Star, pg. D1, July 16, 2004.
4. Richard Gwyn, 'The rich legacy of Eric Kierans' The Toronto Star, May 16, 2004, pg. A13.
5. IBID.
6. Andrea Gordon, 'Kids are being pushed to mature faster than ever' The Toronto star, pg. D2, June 18, 2004.
7. Andrea Gordon, 'Hyper-parents' seek simpler life' The Toronto Star, pg. A1, June 13, 2004.

8. Andrea Gordon, 'Free the children' The Toronto Star, pg. L1, June 12, 2004.
9. Andrea Gordon, 'In search of lost childhood' The Toronto Star, pg. A1, June 11, 2004.
10. Andrea Gordon, 'What are we doing to kids?' The Toronto Star, pg. D1, June 11, 2004.
11. IBID.
12. Andrea Gordon, 'Support helps ease stress felt by students' The Toronto Star, pg. D4, June 11, 2004.
13. Andrea Gordon, 'Parents driven by fear of failure', The Toronto Star, pg. D5, June 11, 2004.

Notes for Chapter Five
The Last Man You'd Want for Mayor

1. Linda McQuaig, 'Black's phoney tax rage', The Toronto Star, Sept. 5, 2004, pg. A13.
2. Laurie Monsebraaten, 'Toronto's mega mayor is down but not necessarily out' The Toronto Star, pg. B1, Jan. 20, 2002.
3. Linwood Barclay, 'It's about time Mayor Miller did something stupid' The Toronto Star, May 3, 2004, pg. E1.
4. IBID.
5. Royson James, 'Talking T.O. in N.Y.C.' The Toronto Star, June 3, 2004, pp. B1 and B5.
6. Royson James, Miller visits NYC's isle oasis, The Toronto Star, June 4, 2004, pp. F1 and F4.
7. IBID.
8. Joseph Hall, 'Towns insist on their fair share', The Toronto Star, August 28, 2004, pg. A10).
9. IBID.
10. IBID.

Notes for Chapter Six
Spoiled Sports

1. Heather Manley, 'Real' fans want more' Letters, The Toronto Star, April 16, 2004, pg. A23.
2. Road trip cheaper than ACC, The Toronto Star. April 4, 2004, pp. A1, A10.
3. Tony Fusco, 'Preserve the gardens' Letters, The Toronto Star, June 17, 2004, pg. A29.
4. IBID.
5. Michael B. Davie, 'Go one-on-one against Balfour. Hockey Hall of Fame has it all' What's On This Summer magazine, The Toronto Star, pg. H3, June 1, 2003.
6. Ben Rayner, 10,000 Juno fans gather, The Toronto Star, April 4, 2004, pg. A10.

Notes for Chapter Seven
Toronto the Good, the Bad and the Ugly

1. Gabe Gonda and Morgan Campbell, 'Girl's injuries called indescribable', The Toronto Star, pg. B1, June 8, 2004.
2. Bill Dunphy In T.O., 'Good people living in a bad place', The Hamilton Spectator, pg. A13, May 14, 2004.
3. Betsy Powell and Peter Small, 'Tragedy over a $10 cover', The Toronto Star, pg. B1, May 28, 2004.
4. IBID.
5. Jordan Heath-Rawlings, 'Hundreds mourn slain youth', The Toronto Star, pg. A1, May 30, 2004.
6. Betsy Powell, '19-year-old charged with crime', The Toronto Star, B1, June 2, 2004.
7. Betsy Powell, '3 more arrested in slaying', The Toronto Star, F1, June 11, 2004.

8. Bill Dunphy in T.O.: 'Random shooting, random love. Outpouring of support for Louise Russo and her family a testament to city's heart' The Hamilton Spectator, pg. A16, May 8, 2004.

9. IBID.

10. Mark Hoult, Letter to the Editor, re: 'Caregiver may never walk again' The Toronto Star, Letters, A19, April 26, 2004.

11. IBID.

12. Shannon Proudfoot, 'Man shot near film festival hangout' The Toronto Star, pg. B2, September 13, 2004.

13. Leslie Ferenc, Cal Millar and Tracy Huffman, 'Downtown suicide probed' The Toronto Star, pg. B3, June 2, 2004.

14. Betsy Powell, 'Midyear unsolved murders tally: 19' The Toronto Star, pg. H1, July 3, 2004.

15. Cal Millar, 'Food terminal worker slain', The Toronto Star, B1, July 8, 2004.

16. Nick Pron and Dale Anne Freed, 'His 'dark secret: Relatives hear Briere's chilling details of Holly's kidnap, brutal attack and murder', The Toronto Star, A1, June 18, 2004.

17. Kevin Donovan, 'The making of a monster: A pedophile turns to murder', The Toronto Star, pp. A1, A8, A9, July 11, 2004.

18. Robert Cribb, 'Knife attacks deliver deadly week: City stabbings kill 5, injure 2', The Toronto Star, pp. A1, A5, July 11, 2004.

19. Frank Calleja, 'Ferrier gets his wish: judge sends him back to jail', The Toronto Star, pg. B2, July 8, 2004.

20. Betsy Powell, 'Gun battle sparks investigations', The Toronto Star, pg. E3, July 9, 2004.

21. Debra Black, 'Mourners call for the killing of blacks to end', The Toronto Star, pg. B7, June 25, 2004.

22. Tarannum Kamlani, Tracy Huffman and Michelle Shephard, 'Man is shot dead, officer hit in park,' The Toronto Star, pg. A1, June 14, 2004.

23. IBID.

24. IBID.

25. Cal Miller, 'Couple awake to horrific scene', The Toronto Star, pg. A4, June 18, 2004.

26. Christian Controneo, 'I'm just going to drive around and kill people', The Toronto Star, pg. A1, June 24, 2004.

27. IBID.

28. Curtis Rush, 'Nightmare' pit bull attack', The Toronto Star, pg. A1, August 29, 2004.

29. IBID.

30. Toronto Star editorial, 'Time for cities to ban pit bulls', The Toronto Star, pg. A18, August 31, 2004.

31. Christian Controneo, 'I'm just going to drive around and kill people', The Toronto Star, pg. A1, June 24, 2004.

32. 'Fighting gun crime', Toronto Star editorial, The Toronto Star, pg. A28, June 24, 2004).

33. IBID.

34. IBID.

35. Bob Mitchell, 'Man facing at least 25 years in prison', The Toronto Star, pg. D3, June 28, 2004.

36. Voices, The Toronto Star, pg. D3, June 28, 2004.

37. Camille Roy, 'Killing of 'good soul' a mystery', The Toronto Star, pg. A6, July 3, 2004.

38. Melissa Godsoe, 'TV tips lead to suspected killer', The Toronto Star, pg. A6, July 3, 2004.

39. Peter Small, 'Victim hunted like 'prey,' two convicted of murder' The Toronto Star, pg. B1, June 9, 2004.

40. Andrew Mills and Leslie Ferenc, 'Padlock park, city urged,' The Toronto Star, pg. B1, August 4, 2004.

41. Jordan Heath-Rawlings, 'Bystanders act quickly to save a life', The Toronto Star, pg. B1, August 3, 2004.

42. Christian Cotroneo, 'Tobacco the new currency of crime', The Toronto Star, pg. A1, August 7, 2004.

43. Cal Millar, 'Landlord-tenant dispute turns ugly' The Toronto Star, pg. B1, August 10, 2004.

44. Melissa Godsoe and William Lin, 'Chief makes arrest himself', The Toronto Star, pp. A1, A12, August 23, 2004.

45. IBID.

46. IBID.
47. Bill Dunphy, 'Toronto is safe, top homicide cop says', The Hamilton Spectator, pg. A11, August 24, 2004.
48. IBID.
49. IBID.
50. Tracey Tyler, 'Judges criticized for pro-black bias' The Toronto Star, pg. A1, August 4, 2004.

Notes for Chapter Eight
Shattered Dreams

1. 'Condo fee hike overdue', Toronto Star editorial, The Toronto Star, pg. A28, June 24, 2004.
2. IBID.
3. IBID.
4. Tony Wong, 'House prices hot and cold', The Toronto Star, pg. D1, April 6, 2004.
5. IBID.
6. Tony Wong, 'Asking: a cool million', The Toronto Star, pg. C1, May 16, 2004.
7. IBID.
8. IBID.
9. IBID.
10. IBID.
11. Bill Dunphy, 'Home buyers in Toronto pay $1 million for no garage, barely a yard. 'These days a million dollars will get you a Rosedale fixer-upper', The Hamilton Spectator, pg. A9, May 7, 2004.
12. IBID.
13. Real estate report, 'What they got', The Toronto Star, pg. C3, August 1, 2004.
14. IBID.

15. Tracy Hanes, 'Lord of the mansions', The Toronto Star, pg. N1, June 12, 2004.

16. Tony Wong, 'How high can it go?' The Toronto Star, pg. C1, June 20, 2004.

17. Real Estate Report, 'What they got', The Toronto Star, pg. C3, June 20, 2004.

18. Tony Wong, 'How high can it go?' The Toronto Star, pg. C1, June 20, 2004.

19. Nancy Devine, 'Estate project borders private woodland', The Toronto Star, pg. N16, June 12, 2004.

20. David Bruser, 'Spring fever' drives up house prices', The Toronto Star, pg. C1, July 7, 2004.

21. Tony Wong, 'Million-dollar deals rise 43% 'It truly defies all logic,' realtor says' The Toronto Star, pg. D1, September 21, 2004.

22. Tony Wong, 'Oakville's Gold Coast, The Toronto Star, pg. C1, August 28, 2004.

23. IBID.

24. IBID.

25. Tony Wong, 'Oakville's Gold Coast, The Toronto Star, pg. C1, August 28, 2004.

26. IBID.

27. Joseph Brean, 'Cottaging is becoming a pastime for the elite' The National Post, May 18, 2004, pg. 1.

28. Tracy Hanes, 'Cottage country facing crunch with noise, crowding' The Toronto Star, pg. N6, July 10, 2004.

29. Anthony Reinhart, 'Old Muskokans taxed out by new money' The Globe and Mail, pg. A13, June 24, 2004.

30. Andrew Mills, 'Couple trades stars above for a roof', The Toronto Star, pg. B1, May 28, 2004.

31. IBID.

32. Debra Black, 'A very beautiful new life for us. Refugees rejoice at sparse home. But high prices worry them' The Toronto Star, pg. B1, August 4, 2004.

33. Nicholas Keung, 'Women face dilemma: Abuse or deportation?' The Toronto Star, pg. B1, August 3, 2004.

34. Catherine Porter, 'Shantytown asks city for portable toilet, garbage pickup', The Toronto Star, pg. B3, August 17, 2004.

35. IBID.

36. IBID.

37. IBID.

38. Carol Goar, 'Room in the heart of the city', The Toronto Star, pg. A22, August 25, 2004.

39. IBID.

40. Thomas A. Axworthy, 'Enough talk: Homeless must become priority…' The Toronto Star, pg. A19, August 9, 2004.

41. IBID.

42. IBID.

43. IBID.

44. IBID.

45. Carol Goar, 'The missing voices in our cities', The Toronto Star, pg. A18, September 3, 2004.

46. Kerry Gillespie, 'Report warns of confining poor to growing 'ghettoes' The Toronto Star, pg. B2, April 6, 2004.

47. Harold Levy, 'Work hard to find for poor single parents' The Toronto Star, pg. F2, September 10, 2004

48. IBID.

49. Paul Moloney, 'Housing approvals signal a city trend. Funds flow to homeless projects. Local dissenters losing their clout', The Toronto Star, pg. B1, August 3, 2004.

50. Allison Dunfield, The number of children living in poverty increased by 73%' The Globe and Mail, June 30, 2003.

51. IBID.

52. Paul Choi, 'Online food bank drive falters Important items in short supply' The Toronto Star, pg. B5, August 27, 2004.

53. William Lin, 'GTA food bank use at its highest' The Toronto Star, pg. B1, August 02, 2004.

54. Debra Black, 'Hungry defy stereotype' The Toronto Star, pg. A16, April 10, 2004.

55. Editorial, 'Action needed on tuition fees' The Toronto Star, pg. A12, September 05, 2004.

56. IBID.

57. IBID.

58. Louise Brown, 'Texts can cost the equivalent of a course tuition Hard-pressed students struggle to cut costs' The Toronto Star, pg. A4, September 13, 2004.

59. Jesse Greener, 'Students need Rae of hope' The Toronto Star, pg. A19, September 07, 2004.

60. IBID.

61. IBID.

Notes for Chapter Nine
The Unliveable City

1. Christian Cotroneo and Vivian Song, 'Smoggy, steamy temperatures knock GTA back on its heels' The Toronto Star, June 9, 2004 pg. B1.

2. Kerry Gillespie, 'Killer pollution increasing: Study' The Toronto Star, pg. A18, July 9, 2004.

3. Elaine Carey, 'Cancer crisis looming in GTA', The Toronto Star, pg. A1, July 3, 2004.

4. Peter Gorrie, 'What lies beneath' The Toronto Star, pg. B1, July 10, 2004.

5. IBID.

6. Ian Urquhart, 'Toronto trash crisis won't go away' The Toronto Star, pg. A17, May 10, 2004.

7. Gail Swainson, 'Vaughn cultivates plan to make old dumps bloom', The Toronto Star, pg. B3, August 4, 2004.

8. ISBN.

9. Christopher Hume, 'Waterfront gets a tangible sign. Promenade gives a hint of the future' The Toronto Star, pg. B3, August 12, 2004.

10. IBID.

11. Christopher Hume, 'Furthering waterfront evolution' The Toronto Star, pg. P2, August 14, 2004.

12.   Christopher Hume, 'Waterfront gets a tangible sign' The Toronto Star, pg. B3, August 12, 2004.

13.   Christopher Hume, 'Bringing the beach downtown', The Toronto Star, pg. B1, July 26, 2004.

14.   IBID.

15.   Brian Levman, 'Significant numbers leaving GTA' The Toronto Star, pg. N8, September 25, 2004.

16.   IBID.

17.   Kelly Toughill, 'Voters 'angry at rural decline', The Toronto Star, pg. A9, June 17, 2004.

18.   John Honderich, 'AMO can't serve Toronto's needs', The Toronto Star, pg. A18, August 31, 2004.

19.   Jane Jacobs, 'Dark Age Ahead' 2004, Random House Canada, 241 pages.

20.   IBID.

21.   IBID.

22.   IBID.

23.   IBID.

24.   Royson James: Urban prophet warns we're drifting to 'dark age' pg. E1, The Toronto Star, May 15, 2004.

25.   IBID.

26.   Alan Broadbent, 'Cities' deal: One size won't fit all', The Toronto Star, September 5, 2004, pg. A13.

27.   IBID.

28.   Tony O'Donohue, 'Water power: Untapped potential: Ontario should replace nuclear stations with more hydro-electric plants as Quebec has done' The Hamilton Spectator, pg. F9, June 12, 2004.

29.   IBID.

30.   IBID.

31.   IBID.

32.   Kerry Gillespie, 'Anti-sprawl plan going to the public', The Toronto Star, pg. B1, July 26, 2004.

33.   Bill Dunphy, 'A fuzzy, if well-intentioned, growth plan', The Hamilton Spectator, pg. A7, July 13, 2004.

34. Christopher Hume, 'Public seating says a lot about our life' The Toronto Star, pg. B1, July 27, 2004.

35. Christopher Hume, 'It may be nature, but it's not natural' The Toronto Star, pg. A3, June 6, 2004.

36. Compiled by Libby Stephens, The Toronto Star, April 3, 2004, pg. K5.

Notes for Chapter Ten
The Main Reason

1. Philip Marchand, 'Toronto the Ignored. Literati leave Big Smoke out in the cold', Toronto Star, November 23, 2002. pg. J4.

2. IBID.

3. Andrew Mills, Parks in decline? Root out those ideas, The Toronto Star, June 4, 2004, pg. F1.

4. IBID.

5. Peter Howell, 'Stars align in Toronto', The Toronto Star, August 25, 2004, pg. F1.

6. IBID.

7. Christian Cotroneo, 'Once starved, now nourishing others' The Toronto Star, pg. B1, September 18, 2004.

8. Royson James, 'Grads gratefully celebrate. Free training a magnet for youth' The Toronto Star, pg. B1, September 1, 2004.

9. Angus Loten, 'Changing their worlds', The Toronto Star, pg. B7, July 26, 2004.

10. Leslie Ferenc, 'Seven Toronto attractions that aren't just for visitors', The Toronto Star, pg. B5, August 8, 2004.

Manor House Publishing Inc.
(905) 648-2193.